Women of the Bible

JACQUES DUQUESNE

Women of the Bible

Flammarion

How beautiful are your feet in their sandals, O prince's daughter!
The curve of your thighs is like the curve of a necklace, work of a master hand.
Your navel is a bowl well rounded with no lack of wine,
your belly a heap of wheat surrounded with lilies.
Your two breasts are two fawns, twins of a gazelle.
Your neck is an ivory tower.
Your eyes, the pools of Heshbon, by the gate of Bath-Rabbim.
Your nose, the Tower of Lebanon, sentinel facing Damascus.
Your head is held high like Carmel, and its hair is as dark as purple;
a king is held captive in your tresses.

How beautiful you are, how charming, my love, my delight!
In stature like the palm tree, its fruit-clusters your breasts.
I have decided, 'I shall climb the palm tree, I shall seize its clusters of dates!'
May your breasts be clusters of grapes, your breath sweet-scented as apples,
and your palate like sweet wine.

(Song of Songs, 7:2–10)

Page 6
Gustave Moreau, *The Song of Songs: the Sulamite* (detail), 1852, private collection

Pages 10–11
Johann Liss, *Adam and Eve Lamenting the Death of Abel*, 1624–25, Galleria dell'Accademia, Venice

introduction

In the famous poem in the Bible known as the "Song of Songs," or "Song of Solomon" (7:2–10), the Lover—the man soon to become the girl's husband—addresses the "Beloved." This glorious paean to love, which exalts not only the beauty of the woman but also her manner of speaking, has surprised many commentators and its place in the Bible has been much discussed.

Jews regard the verses as allegorical, symbolizing the love of God for Israel and the Israelites' adoration of their God. Christians view it as being concerned with the "marriage" between Christ and the Church, or the mystical union of the soul in God. Today, however, many specialists see this strikingly naturalistic text, dating perhaps from the sixth century BCE, as an exaltation of human love.

If the poem's role in the world's bestselling book seems puzzling, it is because in the Bible the purpose of marriage generally seems to be for procreation rather than to celebrate a loving relationship between man and woman.

So it is with Sarai, wife of Abram, the great patriarch, whose tale inaugurates the history of the people of Israel. She was attractive; in fact, very beautiful indeed, to judge by how many coveted her. Even her name means "princess." When young, Abram had lived in Ur at the extreme tip of Mesopotamia, a land lying between two rivers, whose sullen inhabitants felt constantly besieged by evil powers.

Abram's father had in the end settled in the north of this uninspiring stretch of terrain. Abram himself became a venerable elder, rich in both livestock and land, and surrounded by many servants. Abram, however, suffered from one great sorrow: he had no children, as the beautiful Sarai had proved infertile. One day, when he was near the banks of the Euphrates,

Yahweh (God) came down to him. Abram must have been exceptionally pious, since, as the book of Genesis tells us, God charged him with a mission. And what a mission.

> Yahweh said to Abram, "Leave your country, your kindred and your father's house for a country which I shall show you; and I shall make you a great nation, I shall bless you and make your name famous; you are to be a blessing! I shall bless those who bless you, and shall curse those who curse you, and all clans on earth will bless themselves by you." (Genesis 12:1–3).

Abram, even though his ancestors had adored more than one god, did not doubt Yahweh's promise. He started out, abandoning his fields and his home, taking Sarai along, of course (who was by then hardly less ancient than him), with his nephew, Lot, and all his servants. The caravan marched to the country of Canaan, then known for its lucrative purple-dyeing industry. Bordered by the Mediterranean, the Lebanese Mountains, the Valley of the Jordan, and the Dead Sea, it was this territory that was destined to become the "Promised Land."

Leaving a place where he had grown rich, where he was well used to living, and where he had been comfortably settled must have represented quite a wrench for an old man. In responding to a promise made to him that was mysterious if overwhelming, Abram showed his blind faith. But had Yahweh not told him—a man who, after decades of marriage, still had no offspring—that He would make him (him personally, no one else, and not even others with him) into "a great nation"? And, more astonishingly, more incredibly still, the Lord took him "outside [and] said, 'Look up at the sky and count the stars if you can. Just so will your descendants be'" (Genesis 15:5).

This divine initiative, this unlikely promise, and the elect's response—the confidence he shows in his God, the Covenant he concludes with Him—was to transform the history of humanity. And all this was to be accompanied by a new name: Abraham.

This name change frequently occurs for significant characters in the Bible, since for a nomadic people names represented a more important component of identity than perhaps they did for others. In this early period, when signs and symbols were widely employed, a change of name could often be the indicator of a change of destiny: Sarai, too, was subsequently to be renamed Sarah.

In this context, it is crucial to note how the opening books of the Bible comprise a succession of covenants.

The word "covenant" appears for the first time in the remote era of Noah when God-Yahweh "saw that human wickedness was great on earth and that human hearts[1] contrived nothing but wicked schemes all day long [and He] regretted having made human beings on earth and was grieved at heart" (Genesis 6:5). Deciding to erase man from the surface of the Earth, together with all living things, cattle, insects, birds, etc., God retracted his creation and inflicted a collective punishment on all. A surprising step backwards it would seem.

Yahweh, however, had caught sight of a single righteous man, one who acted well and who had faith in Him. And because He found this one loyal individual, this Noah, He afforded creation a second chance, forging a Covenant with all humanity, with all that lives, with all Nature. This Covenant with Noah brought with it rules for men: not to kill, to preserve life, to cohabit in harmony, to unite:

He who sheds the blood of man,
by man shall his blood be shed,
for in the image of God was man created.
(Genesis 9:6).

The Covenant also included a "sign": a "bow"—that is, a rainbow. As Yahweh tells Noah and his son, "'And this,' God said, 'is the sign of the covenant.... I now set my bow in the clouds and it will be the sign of the covenant between me and the earth. When I gather the clouds over the earth and the bow appears in the clouds, I shall recall the covenant between myself and you and every living creature, in a word all living things.'" (Genesis 9:12–16).

At first sight, the Covenant that Yahweh makes with Abraham seems more restrictive: by selecting another unique and worthy man, and his posterity, God chooses a single people, Israel, with which and through which He will participate in the adventure of humanity.

The story of the patriarchs as told by the book of Genesis, whose manner of composition and author remains a mystery, and whose final chapters continue in two divergent versions, does not, of course, amount to "history" in the current, scientific sense of the term. But neither is it just a diverting if moralizing fairy tale. In the final analysis, it is the instructive account of the march that God wants to undertake with humanity. A march to the Kingdom, in the eyes of believers. As Jesus will say: His Father is always at work. Creation is not a divine whim or the work of a few days: it is an ongoing history.

Certainly the Bible of the Hebrews concerns solely what it calls the Lord's Chosen People, and how they were gathered together and liberated from servitude and the shadow of death, so as to attain

true life and freedom. Yet, according to a majority of specialists, this new dispensation does not supersede the universal Covenant concluded with Noah, for the mission of elected people is to pave the way for a humanity reunited in love.

The new sign of the Covenant with Abraham is circumcision, a mark, in the flesh, of the historical continuity of his people. The subsequent Covenant with Moses is more a law, a contract, a legal draft of the relationship between God and His people: the Law. For the people had developed and started questioning the tenets of their beliefs and behavior: they thus had to be provided with rules of conduct, with lessons. This then is the purpose of the Law, the Torah. And the presence of Yahweh among the Israelites is marked by the Ark of the Covenant "in" which Yahweh is and is not—because one cannot, of course, enclose God. He is, then, mysteriously absent and present at the same time, as He will be in the Temple erected by Solomon and the later sanctuary built by Herod. For Christians, finally, Jesus, God incarnate, both God and Man, offers the final seal to the "new and eternal Covenant," as the Catholic priest states at the high point of the Mass, at the elevation of the host.

Considered from this angle, the Covenant, whose foundations were laid by its predecessors, becomes universal once again. Moreover, according to his genealogy composed by the Evangelist Luke (Luke 3:34), Jesus was a descendant of Abraham; because Abraham, as Yahweh had announced, did indeed have a great many progeny.

Yahweh thus fulfilled His promise. Not at once, it is true. The years passed. One year, two, three … even after ten years, Abraham still did not have a child. Furthermore, the aged patriarch and his brethren did not spend these ten years in peace and repose: a famine broke out in the country of Canaan and they had to flee back whence they came.

The Bible features a long series of covenants, but it also tells of wanderings, some simply miserable, others amounting to tentative advances on the path to the Promised Land. And so the little band led by Abraham reached the borders of Egypt, a country—if rumor was to be believed—whose granaries overflowed with grain. Food, at last! But the master is gripped by fear: the Egyptians might steal his beautiful wife and eliminate him as a rival "surplus to requirements." He decides to deploy an astonishing subterfuge: he asks Sarah to "tell them you are my sister, so that they may treat me well because of you and spare my life out of regard for you" (Genesis 12:13). Sarah accepts and the stratagem succeeds: struck by her beauty, Pharaoh's men lead her to their master, who at once enrolls her into his harem. The episode hardly reflects well on Abraham, but his supporters are ready with an explanation; with his back to the wall, he must defend himself with the only weapon available to him—trickery.

In addition, Sarah was actually Abraham's half-sister, as—like him—she was sired by a shadowy figure, a certain Terah. Admittedly, the Evangelist Luke includes him as one of Jesus' ancestors in the lengthy genealogy that has space only for the most pious and respectable characters (Luke 3:34). It turns out, however, that Terah was not so loyal to Yahweh: Joshua, who brought the tribes of Israel into the Promised Land following the death of Moses, accused Abraham and Sarah's father of having served "other gods" (Josha 24:2).

So, as Sarah *is* his half-sister, then what Abraham alleged was not a total lie. But can one marry one's half-sister? Yes, but apparently on one condition, as illustrated in an episode that took place years after the Covenant, when Abraham tried the ruse once more. After leaving Egypt, his troop crossed lands belonging to one of the countless princelings in the region, a certain Abimelech. Once again, Sarah's husband was seized by fear ... and once again he introduces her as his sister! As she is still just as desirable, the king at once conducts her to his palace, but on this occasion Yahweh intervenes. Appearing in a dream to the king that night, He reveals the truth and thus forestalls the threat of adultery.

Abimelech is far from happy about having been misled. He launches into Sarah's husband, who retorts that, in this land where one does not "fear" God, perhaps he might have been assassinated for his wife, adding—and this is interesting—that they are related. "Anyway, she really is my sister, my father's daughter though not my mother's, besides being my wife" (Genesis 20:12). It thus seems that the customs of the period permitted a man's marrying the daughter of his father, but that of his mother is out of bounds—a rule underpinned by the more rigorous taboo on mother–son incest observable in a great number of societies.

The story teaches us something else, too, which is of still greater importance since it relates to the attitude of Yahweh. In the Egyptian affair, who was punished? Pharaoh, whom Yahweh struck with "severe plagues on Pharaoh and his household because of Abram's wife Sarai" (Genesis 12:17). Pharaoh, thus enlightened, gives Abraham his wife back and has the couple conducted out of the country, accompanied by slaves and maidservants, camels, asses, and she-asses—all gifts to the cheat. Pharaoh then was not such a bad sort, unless of course he was guided solely by fear.

In the second episode, however, in which Abraham misleads Abimelech, Yahweh does not intervene afterwards, but on the first evening, derailing Abraham's trick and sparing the innocent Abimelech. Puzzlement as to this difference in treatment is dispelled by the information given by Yahweh to Abimelech: "Now send the man's wife back; for he is a prophet and can intercede on your behalf for your life" (Genesis 20:7). Abraham then does not become prophet in the usual biblical sense of the term; he is a prophet because he has a privileged relationship with God, because he is invulnerable and able to intermediate and so save lives.

Yahweh's change of attitude between the Egyptian episode and the fate of Abimelech can then be explained by the new Covenant. "When Abram was ninety-nine years old," says the Bible, "Yahweh appeared to him and said, 'I am El Shaddai [God]. Live in my presence, be perfect, and I shall grant a covenant between myself and you, and make you very numerous'" (Genesis 17:1).

The rule thus goes further than the one laid down for Noah: now the emphasis is on being irreproachable. And the significance of the sign of the Covenant, circumcision, should not be underestimated. What Yahweh requires of Abraham is to sacrifice part of his skin, but not just any old part: a piece from the member that makes man a man. The loss of this scrap of male flesh can be compensated for only by relations with the flesh of woman. So man is not everything. "It is not right that the man should be alone. I shall make him a helper," God had already said on creating Eve (Genesis 2:18). This is then an important factor for understanding the place and role of women in the Bible.

Just as Yahweh tells the prophet: "And you are no longer to be called Abram; your name is to be Abraham, for I am making you father of many nations. I shall make you exceedingly fertile" (Genesis 17:5–6). He commands him furthermore: "As regards your wife Sarai, you must not call her Sarai, but Sarah. I shall bless her and moreover give you a son by her" (Genesis 17:15–16).

Is then Sarah's function limited to procreation, to just finally giving Abraham the child he has craved for so long? Is the role of the woman solely to ensure the survival and spread of this little band? One might well think so reading the following episodes relating the impatience of patriarchs whose wives—whether by chance or misfortune—turn out barren.

Let us go back to the very first woman, to Eve, who is usually regarded as deplorable. Her story is well known: Yahweh put the man to sleep, took out one of his ribs and "closed the flesh up again forthwith."[2] Then He molded the rib into woman and brought her to the man, who exclaimed: "This one at last is bone of my bones and flesh of my flesh! She is to be called Woman, because she was taken from Man" (Genesis 2:23). In Hebrew, man is called "Ich" and woman "Ichah." By giving the name Ichah to his wife, Adam places her on an equal footing with him. He regards her as a person with whom he will maintain a special, close relationship. It is only when the couple is driven out of paradise that the woman is called "Eve"—"Havah" in Hebrew. "The man named his wife 'Eve' because she was the mother of all those who live" (Genesis 3:20).

So negative has Eve's image since become that this obviously important role is all too often skirted over. Yet the two names allotted to her (by Adam) in Genesis seem to indicate that she combines femininity (Ichah) and motherhood (Havah).

Woman, then, is not just the gender through which man ensures his descent. True, from the very start of her life in the couple, Eve delights in this role: "I have acquired a man with the help of Yahweh" (Genesis 4:1), she exclaims when carrying her first child. But no less relevantly, her jubilation was misplaced, as she gave birth to Cain.[3] Yet it should not be forgotten that the first and only sentence put in the mouth of Eve after her exile from the "Garden of Eden" expresses pride in becoming a mother.

From Abraham and Sarah onward, the book of Genesis, indeed the whole of the Old Testament, foregrounds the history of the Hebrews. Its role is to proclaim the existence of the one and only God throughout the world; but the Hebrews were just a tiny population. Thus, when God makes his Covenant with Abraham, the prophet feels devastatingly alone. Even though Yahweh explicitly tells him, "Look up at the sky and count the stars if you can. Just so will your descendants be" (Genesis 15:5), to take such a promise at face value requires immense faith: hence sometimes Abraham ends by doubting and moaning, or showing fear. And the same will apply to many other patriarchs after him. At the head of a small, often wandering people, they became obsessed by fatherhood, by the need to "go forth and multiply," a desire that serves to mark deeply the place and functions allotted to woman.

For centuries, this had been true of nomadic or seminomadic peoples, and in a more general way throughout the rural world. A woman was not seen as being capable of working to the same degree as a man. Neither could she be of great help in the battles that often raged between these tribes and small local

kingdoms. Moreover, she was not thought much of a hunter. Quite naturally, therefore, the authors of the Bible describe how Yahweh addressed the patriarchs, and them alone. And, just as naturally, these men never consulted their wives when it came to taking serious decisions such as setting out for some distant, unknown destination. And so Abraham fails to consult Sarah. Other leaders of this people turn to "the ancients," or their sons, but not to their wives.[4]

Yet often the women take the initiative and don't allow themselves to be taken in. In that seminal text, the Decalogue, the Ten Commandments handed down to Moses, one finds a phrase that places woman on a par with man: "Honor your father and your mother" (Exodus 20:12). But the precept concerns *mothers*, woman as she ensures the survival of the Hebrews, an absolute obsession, as we have outlined, among all those who are responsible for that.

One episode is particularly significant in this respect. It relates to the stay of the Hebrews in Egypt, but not that of Abraham and his little group, but a later one, well after the death of Abraham, at a time when they were slaves and had become far more numerous. The pharaoh of that era, much more bloodthirsty than his predecessor, ordered all the male offspring of Israel to be thrown into the Nile, sparing the daughters, who were later to be handed over to the locals (for Egypt, too, needed mothers). The task of killing the newborns was entrusted to two Jewish midwives. "But the midwives were God-fearing women and did not obey the orders of the king of Egypt, but allowed the boys to live" (Exodus 1:17). The furious pharaoh summoned them, of course, but they were quick-witted enough to answer that the women of Israel, being more vigorous than their Egyptian counterparts, delivered

themselves before the midwives had the chance to get to them. Yahweh, as the Bible puts it, fortified their courage. And how? "He gave them families of their own," of course. Pharaoh, however, persevered and ordered his people to hurl all the newborn of Israel "into the river." So it was that a woman of the house of Levi gave birth to a boy. The text of the book of Exodus emphasizes how pretty the newborn was, as if the mother therefore had even more reason to want to save him: "seeing what a fine child he was, she kept him hidden for three months" (Exodus 2:2) (no father appears in this story at all).

Moses—for he is the hero of the tale—was thus saved by no fewer than three women. Firstly by his mother, who, unable to conceal him for too long, lays him in a papyrus basket coated with bitumen and pitch, and floats him in the reeds on the banks of the Nile. Then by an elder sister, who, from a safe distance, keeps watch over him. And finally, by the daughter of Pharaoh, who, in a well-known scene, sees the basket, frets about the fate of the infant, and eventually returns him to his own mother to be nursed. Female solidarity thus existed, to an extent counterbalancing the absolutism of male power.

Male preeminence was not, however, the exclusive prerogative of the people of the Bible, of course. In the fourth century BCE, the great Aristotle, who studied, inter alia, sexual difference, began by noting that men's brains were larger than women's. Having reviewed all the parts of the human body, the Greek philosopher concluded: "Women are by nature weaker and colder, and their nature should be considered as a natural defect." That is to say, woman is a "lack": for instance, with her, everything is smaller. Breasts are larger in females than in males, as Aristotle is forced to concede, but "compared to male pectorals, these are spongy protuberances; always soft, they can fill with milk, but are quickly emptied."[5] The maternal body is a kind of vessel, an inert substance; the only thing she wants is the "principle of soul." It is also the father alone who transmits the archetype of the species. Here Plato had preceded Aristotle: for him, too, the **mother** was a material "vessel" and no more.

On the other hand, in biblical texts that also often treat woman as a kind of surrogate, intellectual or spiritual inferiority is not emphasized. It is true that in Mesopotamia, whence the Hebrews came, women enjoyed various traditional and customary rights, notably that of choosing the name of their infants, which was then of great significance—especially, as we have seen, for the nomadic people that the Hebrews became when ordered by Yahweh to set off in quest of the Promised Land.

The Bible abounds in pedigrees; this is surely because nomads cannot specify place of residence or even birthplace on their "identity card." However, the near totality of biblical genealogies runs down the male line, from father to son or from son to father: X son of Y, son of Z, etc. Nonetheless, in that part of the Bible that Christians call the New Testament, the genealogy of Jesus, as established by Matthew and set down at the opening of his gospel, quotes four women: Tamar, Ruth, "the wife of Uriah" (that is, Bathsheba, a woman of **foreign origin** to whom we will return), and finally, of course, Mary.

The reason is that the importance ascribed to mothers has over time increased. As for a woman's right to choose the name of her baby, it appears on several occasions in the Bible, even in the opening pages of the book of Genesis: Eve, after the death of Abel, brings a third son into the world, and it is she who gives him the name of Seth (Genesis 4:25). It is true that, in the following verse, Seth chooses the name of Enosh for his son. But generally it is the woman who selects the name. In some cases, this privilege may extend to the group of matrons attending the **childbirth**. Hence for David's grandfather: "And the women of the neighborhood gave him a name … and they called him Obed. This was the father of Jesse, the father of David" (Ruth 4:17). Then, in the gospel according to St. Luke, when Elizabeth is confined with the child who will become John the Baptist, her entourage wants to call the child Zachariah, but the mother protests: "No, he will be called John" (Luke 1:60). The controversy aroused is dispelled by consultation with the father, who ratifies his wife's choice. In a third type of case, the biblical text sometimes states that the father and mother chose the name in tandem. This would seem to have happened (though here translations differ) for Esau, firstborn son of Isaac and Rebecca (Genesis 25:25), best known for having abandoned his birthright to his brother, Jacob (Genesis 25: 29–34).

It can obviously be no coincidence that all these texts by various authors are at pains to record exactly who—out of father, mother, entourage, or Yahweh himself—chose the name of the child. The salient point is the fact that the name implies some future vocation or call: Abram becomes Abraham at the time of Covenant, while Jesus gives new names to a number of his companions.

The role of women in selecting a name is then indicative of their **power**. At the time of the patriarchs, moreover, as it is related in the book of Genesis, it seems that women possess a dwelling place of their own, their personal tent.

The marriage between Isaac and Rebecca (Rebekah), heralded by any number of adventures and portentous signs, is related as follows: "Then Isaac took her into his tent. He married Rebekah and made her his wife. And in his love for her, Isaac was consoled for the loss of his mother" (Genesis 24:67). Sarah had then taken her own tent while she was still married to Abraham, who admittedly had "taken" the maidservant Hagar before driving her away. In passing, it should be noted that the verb "to take" does not mean just sexual intercourse: it also implies true possession.

Prior to wedlock, unmarried girls seem to have enjoyed a measure of freedom. Working as shepherdesses, some kept watch over the herds in the countryside. Thus the "beloved" in the Song of Songs addresses her betrothed:

Come, my love, let us go to the fields.
We will spend the night in the villages,
and in the early morning we will go to the vineyards
(Song of Songs 7:12).

But such liberty is of course carefully monitored, as the same poem underlines:

Ah, why are you not my brother,
nursed at my mother's breast!
Then if I met you out of doors,
I could kiss you without people thinking ill of me
(Song of Songs 8:1).

In reality, a young girl had little choice as to the betrothed, who was chosen by her parents, very often before she had even attained puberty.

Her relations—effectively her father, together with her elder brothers, whose power was substantial among Semitic peoples—took part in negotiations preceding the wedding, which focused on what is still called, in many societies, the dowry or bride price—that is, not what her parents give to the future wife, but the converse: money paid by the suitor. This is because the girl, as an instrument of procreation and looked on as a kind of breeding animal, possesses—to put it in bald terms—a "commercial" value. Among the Mesopotamians, with whom Abraham and his predecessors lived, the fiancé had to hand over money to his future father-in-law, the sum, called the *terhatu*, often being the result of discussions between the parties, or sometimes precisely fixed by law. Once the people of Israel was constituted as such, the name of this practice changed; at that juncture the bride-price became known as the *mohar*; but the tradition subsisted, to the benefit of brothers no less than fathers.

When Isaac's wife-to-be, Rebecca, comes across the servant of Abraham who is looking for a daughter of her race, she hurries off to the "house of her mother" (distinct, then again, from that of her father) to announce the meeting. Her brother, Laban, no paragon of virtue, takes things in hand and starts negotiations. He, like his father—and even taking precedence over him, if the text is followed literally—has to give his agreement. In an appendix to the Song of Songs (8:8), already, at a very early stage, brothers ponder the role they must play in the matter: "Our sister is little: her breasts are not yet formed. What shall we do for our sister on the day she is spoken for?" And they are concerned to protect her virginity because obviously the *mohar* for a virgin is far superior.

With the business concluded, the period of betrothal proper begins: at this point, the engagement is more or less definitive. The fiancée does not cohabit with her betrothed, but is nonetheless regarded as a married woman. This is the situation that Mary and Joseph were in at the time of the Annunciation.

After the wedding ceremony, which follows quickly after the conclusion of the engagement, the young woman of course passes under the total authority of her husband. According to the Halakhah,[6] in religious matters wives stand in the same category as slaves[7] and children, so that she cannot testify in lawsuits, nor study the Law (to which she is however subject), and she is separated from the menfolk at the Temple of Jerusalem and at the synagogue.

For long periods of her life, a woman is regarded as "impure" (purity being then an obsession and its opposite as a kind of contagion), in particular during menstruation. At certain times, this periodic "impurity" meant she had to be kept in isolation. The couple could then not have sexual relations and, as the heavy bleeding at the birth of a child is comparable to her menses, mothers remain in a state of impurity for seven days after birth if the baby was a boy, and fourteen if a girl.

To this were added the "days of purification," during which a new mother could not enter the sanctuary, and at the end of which she had to make a sacrifice; the gospel of Luke (2:21–24), which relates how Mary fulfilled this duty following the birth of Jesus states that, as she was poor, her offering amounted to a pair of turtledoves or two young doves.

The wise men (specialists in the Law), who commented on all these regulations, recalled Eve's sin and stressed the psychological benefits to be had in the context of married life that, they alleged, would only grew stronger through regular abstinence.

Counterbalancing these provisions, which Judaism has, in the main, since thrown off, women within the family have been elevated to the status of "queens with the hearth." The resulting attitude, as one can read in the pages of *The Encyclopaedia of Judaism*,[8] was an extremely ambivalent one: woman is treated as a lower being on the ritual level, but she is simultaneously hailed and elevated, in the later biblical era, as the "female incarnation of wisdom."

It should also be noted that rabbinical law tended to gradually extend the rights of married women. As the rabbi and historian Josy Eisenberg has written, "If a husband becomes poor, this must not have a deleterious effect on the living standards he had promised [his wife]: the number of her maidservants, for instance. He cannot refuse her conjugal rights … [and] must honor his wife at least once a week, except if his profession takes him traveling; in which case, caravanners have to make an appearance every month and mariners every six months! This vigilance and attentiveness is alone enough to show the extent to which sexual relations were judged not only permissible but important. In addition, a husband cannot force himself upon his wife."[9]

When it comes to divorce, however, it is the husband who has the upper hand: he can repudiate his wife, but the corollary is not allowed, whereas it had been among the Babylonians, with whom the future Israelites had lived at the time of Abraham. A husband is obliged to justify his decision in a written text, but the reasons adduced can be ambiguously expressed. A woman may remarry (after a gap of ninety-one days), but never with her first husband, because remarriage makes her "impure" in his eyes. This is a rule with which David did not comply; but then he was a king.

Much later, the Talmud (the digest of commentaries on the Law compiled in the first centuries of the

Christian era) modified certain arrangements concerning divorce, including the provision that a court could force a man to grant his wife a divorce if he had not given her a child after ten years of wedlock: so the desire for offspring was now recognized as legitimate for the opposite sex too.

The finest biblical "portrait" of an ideal woman probably appears at the conclusion of Proverbs, a book composed between the eighth and fifth centuries BCE that contains the beliefs and writings of the sages of Israel. An acrostic where the first letters in each verse form the Hebrew alphabet, entitled "The Capable Woman," celebrates this perfect specimen. She is, needless to say, first and foremost a mother (Proverbs 31:10–31).

> The truly capable woman—who can find her?
>   She is far beyond the price of pearls.
> Her husband's heart has confidence in her,
>   from her he will derive no little profit.
> Advantage and not hurt
>   she brings him all the days of her life.
> She selects wool and flax,
>   she does her work with eager hands.
> She is like those merchant vessels,
>   bringing her food from far away.
> She gets up while it is still dark
>   giving her household their food,
> giving orders to her serving girls.
>   She sets her mind on a field, then she buys it;
> with what her hands have earned she plants a vineyard.
>   She puts her back into her work
> and shows how strong her arms can be.
>   She knows that her affairs are going well;
> her lamp does not go out at night.
>   She sets her hands to the distaff,
> her fingers grasp the spindle.

> She holds out her hands to the poor,
> she opens her arms to the needy.
> …
> She weaves materials and sells them,
> she supplies the merchant with sashes.
> She is clothed in strength and dignity,
> she can laugh at the day to come.
> When she opens her mouth, she does so wisely;
> on her tongue is kindly instruction.
> She keeps good watch on the conduct of her house-
>   hold,
> no bread of idleness for her.
> Her children stand up and proclaim her blessed,
> her husband, too, sings her praises:
> "Many women have done admirable things,
> but you surpass them all."
> Charm is deceitful, and beauty empty;
> the woman who fears Yahweh is the one to praise.
> Give her a share in what her hands have worked for,
> and let her works tell her praises at the city gates.

"Charm is deceitful, and beauty empty." How different from the Song of Songs!

Yet the words that are chosen to describe the most important women in the Bible show that attitudes were never quite so clear-cut.

mothers

But God said to [Abraham], "Do not distress yourself on account of the boy and your slave-girl. Do whatever Sarah says, for Isaac is the one through whom your name will be carried on, but the slave-girl's son I shall also make into a great nation, for he too is your child." Early next morning, Abraham took some bread and a skin of water and, giving them to Hagar, put the child on her shoulder and sent her away.
(Genesis 21, 12–14)

Mothers

Sarah | Hagar | The daughters of Lot | Rebecca | Rachel | Leah | Tamar | Hannah

It is certainly a curious phenomenon: the patriarchs are obsessed by their need to procreate, but their wives are often sterile. It starts with Sarah; then comes Rebecca, the wife of Isaac, who had to wait for twenty years before giving birth, although then it was to twins, Jacob and Esau. In a marriage that takes the form of a soap opera in which female rivalry plays a key role, Jacob encounters the same setback with his wife Rachel.

Finally, though, Jacob, from four different women (two wives who were also sisters, and two serving girls) fathered no fewer than thirteen children: twelve boys, and a daughter, Dinah, whose life was singularly unhappy. The descendants of the twelve sons were to grow into the twelve tribes of Israel.

The status of the handmaidens was ambiguous; their role seemed to hover somewhere between that of wife and concubine. Even if they did not invariably share the master's bed, they were highly considered and partook of the family meal on feast days. But of course they remained in service.

An example of this is Hagar (Agar), Sarah's Egyptian maidservant. Abraham's wife, sorely troubled by her sterility and anxious to ensure her husband's progeny, ended up pushing her maid into the patriarch's bed. But the rest of the story is far from edifying. The book of Genesis contains two varying accounts. In the first (Genesis 16:3–16), as soon as the maidservant gets pregnant, the women enter into competition. With some reason, it seems, Sarah finds that Hagar is taking on airs and that Abraham is neglecting his wife a little. She complains to Abraham, but he does not seem unduly worried by the situation. Sarah seizes her chance and mistreats her servant to the point that Hagar has to take flight.

Luckily, Yahweh shows greater concern. He orders Hagar to return home, with instructions to tell her mistress that she is to give birth to a son whom she is to call Ishmael (meaning "God hears") and he will have many descendants.[1] Hagar obeys and makes her way back to Abraham. By then Abraham was eighty-six years old. Three years later, Yahweh concludes the Covenant with him and announces that Sarah will soon give him a son in her turn. A year afterwards, Isaac is born.

The months pass and the boys grow; at a feast, Sarah gazes on them playing together, and, concerned at the attitude of the elder child, asks her husband to send both Ishmael and his mother away.[2] Though the proposal is far from Abraham's liking, Yahweh requires that he "do whatever Sarah says" on this front, reassuring him that "the slave-girl's son I shall also make into a great nation, for he too is your child." Abraham thus drives the child out. Then, when Hagar, in despair and without water on the road, turns away from her son so she will not have to see him die, God fulfills His promise. He shows her a well, adding: "I shall make him into a great nation" (Genesis 21:8–21). Ishmael has since been thought of as the ancestor of the Arabs and is venerated as such.

Yahweh thus constantly intervenes in the history of the patriarchs and their wives, as well as in that of surrogate partners such as Hagar. And it seems that the authors of these texts place such insistence on sterility precisely so as to underline these cases of divine intervention. Their intention is to show how the Chosen People would never have existed had Yahweh not helped them overcome the many obstacles in their path. Abraham would have had no descendants and the line would have been snuffed out.

Even more crucially, they stress how a birth presupposes joint action between God and a human couple: for the will of both parties ensures not only an individual's future, but also that of all humanity— that is, History itself. The human act of will, however, pertains as much—and even perhaps primarily—to women as men. This is the case with Abraham, almost a hundred years old and still without child, to whom Sarah gives Hagar as a provisional "spouse"—no easy decision, to judge by the way in which she subsequently abuses her maidservant.

For, if a desire for motherhood constructs the future, it is also constitutive of woman, a fact that transpires in all these stories, from Sarah to the daughters of Lot. These are women who take matters into their own hands, who fight, who harbor few scruples as to the means to be employed to ensure their man his descent. This is indeed proof of their excellence.

Perhaps without realizing it, they are seen as the midwives of history. At the time of the patriarchs, these fearsome females, these mothers of the Bible, not only produce children that ensure a future for their people, they also intervene in the affairs of their husbands, and sometimes even challenge Yahweh Himself.

Unable to face being barren, Sarah, for instance, reproaches Yahweh for her condition, alleging that it is His fault she is sterile and He who has prevented her becoming pregnant.[3] He has been promising

sarah and hagar

Abraham descendants for years and nothing has happened! It is she who finds a solution in the law of Mesopotamia, a country they left so many years before: an infertile wife is allowed to give her husband one of her maidservants and acknowledge the children born of this union as her own.

But Sarah has only fulfilled half the law's demands, and, even before Ishmael is born, she becomes jealous of her servant girl. Three years later, Yahweh renews His promise: He "will bless" Sarah, i.e., she will have a son, who will have offspring, and she will thus become a mother for the "kings of the people." The venerable Abraham welcomes Yahweh as it is meet to do, but he also cannot stop sniggering, as Sarah, now aged ninety, has, of course, long since ceased menstruating. Yahweh, however, goes so far as to provide a name for the promised son: "You will call him Isaac." (Genesis 17-19). In Hebrew "Yihac-[el]" means "[God] laughs." Yahweh thus can have a sense of humor. But, if laughter dominates in this story (in contrast the early centuries of Christianity would see such a subject as sinful[4]), what kind of hilarity is it? If Yahweh's is surely joyous and amused, Sarah's is harder to interpret, since she, too, is amused at this annunciation.

When Yahweh returns in the company of two angels to see Abraham, Sarah prepares them flatbreads. She then retires, but keeps within earshot; while they eat at the foot of a tree, she listens at the entrance to the tent, and hears the chief guest (Yahweh and His companions appear in the shape of men) state that He will return the following year and that she will then have a son. The aged Sarah, unaware of the identity of these three figures, laughs skeptically in the corner: "Now that I am past the age of childbearing, and my

husband is an old man, is pleasure to come my way again?" (Genesis 18:12). Yahweh seeks her out and she emerges from the shadows: "'Nothing is impossible for Yahweh. I shall come back to you at the same time next year and Sarah will have a son.' Sarah said, 'I did not laugh,' lying because she was afraid. But he replied, 'Oh yes, you did laugh'" (Genesis 18:14–15). He then departs, followed by His two companions. Now He is less in the mood for laughter, as He is going to Sodom, where, as is well known, the inhabitants had adopted sexual practices that He condemns.

Abraham accompanies the travelers a bit of the way. Yahweh, since He has made a covenant with the patriarch, thinks it right to inform him as to His intentions: He is off to destroy Sodom and Gomorrah. Abraham negotiates clemency for the cities. Haggling, he proposes that they should be spared if they contain at least fifty "upright men," then forty, then thirty.

This is followed by another story in which the desire for progeny is once again at the center, together with the capacity of women to deploy the most debatable methods to satisfy it. The daughters of Abraham's nephew, Lot, are of this stock: the two men, having gone together to Egypt and shared land and property, had parted company. Lot now lived in Sodom; and precisely because he was just and upright

The daughters of Lot

he offered hospitality to two strangers who presented themselves at the gates of the city, ignorant of the fact that they were angels sent by Yahweh to destroy it.

But the rumor spread like wildfire. From early on that night, a large crowd assembled outside Lot's house with one idea in mind: to "have intercourse with" the newcomers (Genesis 19:5). The rumpus can scarcely be imagined: there were, as the Bible text puts it, "The men of Sodom both young and old, all the people without exception" (Genesis 19:4).

The courageous Lot then leaves his house and makes a bizarre proposal to the crowd. Do not commit an evil act, he pleads: "Look, I have two daughters who are virgins. I am ready to send them out to you, for you to treat as you please, but do nothing to these men since they are now under the protection of my roof" (Genesis 19: 8). Delivering up his daughters, who are, moreover, virgins (that supreme quality) to a sex-crazed mob to keep his unknown visitors from harm—this madcap scheme goes well beyond the obligations of hospitality. But the crowd refuses, and this bizarre trade-off on the lesser of two evils falls flat. Grievous punishments, however, await the mob. Lot returns safe and sound and his two guests strike the assailants with blindness, so that, as the Bible says, they are unable to find the entrance to the house: this enraged rabble is neither strong nor particularly bright.

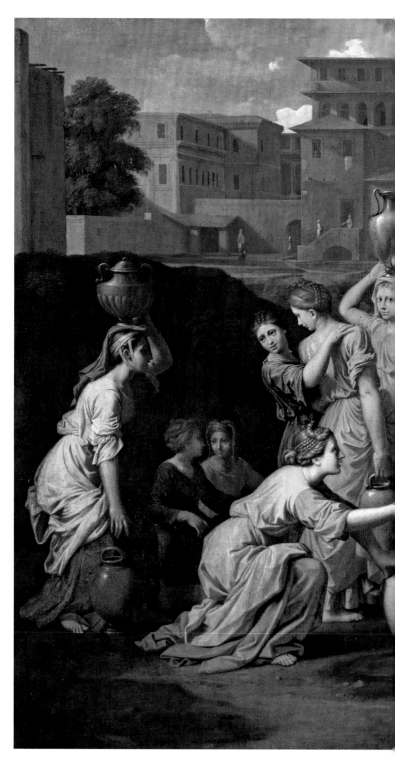

The following day, as dawn breaks, Lot, after much hesitation, flees with his wife and daughters.[5] Yahweh then makes a torrent of fire and sulfur (brimstone) rain down on Sodom and its neighbor Gomorrah. Lot and his family are accompanied by angels who urge them to run on without looking back. Failing to observe this instruction, perhaps because she cannot bear to leave their property behind, Lot's wife is at once transformed into a statue of salt. The old man, however, takes refuge in a cave with his two virgin daughters. Seeing that there are no men left in the land (among a people where to be a woman means being a mother), they are reluctant to abandon their hope of becoming complete women. The elder girl then proposes: "Come on, let us ply our father with wine and sleep with him. In this way we can preserve the race by our father" (Genesis 19:32). She is clearly aware that Lot, if he ever got wind of what was afoot, would recoil. But, ignoring a universal taboo, she is prepared to commit incest, and her sister does the same the next day.

With heavy heart, Lot had resolved to hand them over to a crowd of Sodomites for an orgy, yet they commit with him what their people regarded as a capital sin. But the ruse worked: the elder had a son she called Moab, the younger another boy she named Ben-Ammi, and their descendants, the Moabites and the Ammonites, were often to cross swords with Israel. But, even from the line of Moab, regarded since the time of Moses as outsiders, there appears in the list of Jesus's ancestors in Matthew's genealogy (Matthew 1:5) a certain Ruth, a woman who abandoned father, mother, and country to go up to Bethlehem.

The march of the people is one of twists and turns, then: though his ways are straight, the Lord employs crooked paths. The story of Isaac demonstrates the same fact.

Isaac is the second of the great patriarchs from whom the people of the Lord were descended. His existence was certainly necessary, but he seems little more than a stepping stone, the "son of Abraham and father of Jacob," as if there were not much more to add about him. He has even sometimes been described as a "patriarch of transition" between two spiritual giants: he is one of the weaker links along the chain, but at least he existed.

Isaac, on whose story the Bible does not linger, married a woman of strong character who was not afraid of infringing rules and regulations: Rebecca. Inevitably Rebecca was extremely comely, too, and, no less inevitably, infertile: sterility in the Bible is never a male problem.

Old Abraham, afraid that his son Isaac might marry a depraved and idolatrous woman of Canaan, had sent his servant, Eliezer, to find a girl of his own race in Haran, where he had once lived. On arriving there, Eliezer spotted some girls drawing water for their camels from a spring. His mounts, after their long journey, were parched. He thus made an agreement with Yahweh: "I shall say to one of the girls, 'Please lower your pitcher and let me drink.' And if she answers, 'Drink, and I shall water your camels too,' let her be the one you have decreed for your servant Isaac" (Genesis 24:14).

Rebecca was the first to run up to him. She hurried off back to the spring to fill her jug and give him water. Dazzled, Abraham's servant asked her whether her family might allow him to lodge with his camels. Without even seeking the opinion of her parents, she promises him they will be able to. Then Eliezer blesses Yahweh who, as it were, has "arranged" matters so well, as the girl's father and her brother Laban note

submissively: "This is from Yahweh; it is not for us to say yes or no to you" (Genesis 24:50). Bowing to the inevitable, they seem unenthusiastic; though this does not prevent them spending part of the night drinking with Abraham's envoy. The very next day, then, Eliezer sets out, taking the radiant Rebecca along with him, accompanied by her nurse, maidservants, and camels.

When, walking through the countryside, Isaac sees the little caravan draw up, he could hardly have expected what was going to happen. He then "took her into his tent. He married Rebekah and made her his wife. And in his love for her, Isaac was consoled for the loss of his mother" (Genesis 24:67).

Yahweh is a constant presence in the story of Rebecca. First of all, when Isaac eventually has to accept that his wife is definitely infertile, he beseeches his God and his wish is granted: Rebecca becomes pregnant with twins. They fight in her belly, though and, worried, she too consults Yahweh, who explains that each child represents a different people. At their birth, the first to emerge is redheaded and very hairy: he is named Esau. The second keeps a firm grip on his brother—in the literal meaning of the expression in that he holds on to his heel; he will be called Jacob, as "*aqeb*" means "heel."[6] The two infants are as different as can be. The apple of his father's eye, Esau dreams only of racing through the woods and hunting. As for Jacob, he meditates quietly in the tent. He is his mother's favorite, and that of Yahweh, too, as will become evident. In Rebecca he has a staunch ally.

The first episode is well known: Esau returns from the hunt starving and exhausted, feeling dead on his feet. His twin brother seizes his opportunity and swindles him out of his birthright. Esau falls for the

Rebecca

trick and obtains as compensation a piece of bread and the famous "mess of potage" (lentil stew).

Then comes the second stage: the aging Isaac has by now almost lost his sight. Afraid he is nearing the end, he asks Esau to go out and hunt the game he is so fond of. Rebecca, who is unhappy at the fact her firstborn has taken a pair of Hittite women as wives, overhears it all.[7] She calls forth Jacob and orders him to find among their immense herds of goat (patriarchs are always wealthy) two of the finest kids so she can make an "appetizing dish" for his father; he will present this to him, and Isaac, unable to tell Jacob from his preferred son, will bless him. Initially rather reticent, Jacob does as he is bidden. Rebecca then dresses him in Esau's most splendid garments, and, covering his hands and neck with the goatskin, turns him into his brother. And the ruse succeeds. When Isaac expresses astonishment as to the speed with which his son has found his quarry, Jacob compounds the lie, explaining that Yahweh helped him flush them out. When Esau returns from the hunt, as in the last act of a finely crafted play, the scurrilous trick is exposed. But there is no going back now. All the more since—and all feel this is the case—Yahweh seems well pleased. Isaac, dying, thus blesses Jacob once more.

Rebecca meanwhile prudently advises her favorite to keep out of Esau's way for a time; she suggests he take refuge with his uncle Laban. Jacob gets going; en route he encounters Yahweh at the end of a dream in which he sees angels climbing up an immense ladder reaching up to heaven. On that occasion, Yahweh promises him plentiful progeny; just as He had previously done for Abraham. "Be sure, I am with you; I shall keep you safe wherever you go" (Genesis 28:15).

As a confirmation of Yahweh's special regard, this pronouncement almost amounts to another fully fledged covenant. Jacob, however, can hardly believe it. It can happen that a man finds it hard to understand and women get the point faster: the wives of the patriarchs are no paragons of virtue, but Yahweh is not above joining forces with them, and sometimes they sense more quickly than their husbands the path He has in mind for His people.

This is the case with Rachel, who was "shapely and beautiful" (Genesis 29:17). Daughter of Laban, brother of Rebecca, she was thus Jacob's cousin, and it was she whom Jacob first came across, while she was leading her father's herd to the well. Laban then greeted his nephew enthusiastically ("You are indeed my bone and flesh!").

Rachel and Leah

He agrees to Jacob's suit for Rachel, with the proviso that the young man work for him, free, for seven years before the nuptials: "Laban replied, 'It is better for me to give her to you than to a stranger; stay with me'" (Genesis 29:19). Hardly encouraging!

Jacob was cunning, and should have been wary, but he was blinded by love for Rachel. So, he accepted, and the seven years, as the Bible story has it, "seemed to him like a few days because he loved her so much" (Genesis 29:20). A patient fiancé indeed.

The long wait having come to an end, Jacob reminds Laban of his promise. Rachel's father sends out the invitations at once and throws a banquet. But who does he lead into Jacob's tent? His elder daughter, Leah, whose sight was poor. As the bride had to wear a veil for seven days, the ceremony lasted until the wedding night proper. Jacob does not realize the trick, and thus finds himself coupled to the elder daughter: "But when night came, he took his daughter Leah and brought her to Jacob, and he slept with her." The two men argue, Laban alleging that custom holds that elder daughters should marry first.[8] He is, though, prepared to hand Rachel over to Jacob too, after another week of wedding ceremonies, provided that he promises to work for his dear uncle for a further seven years.

Eventually, then, "Jacob slept with Rachel too, and he loved Rachel more than Leah" (Genesis 29:30). Jealousy between the two sisters was then bound to break out. Leah proved infertile, but, on her entreaty, Yahweh intervened and she had a son, Reuben. Her delight was twofold: "Now my husband will love me," she thinks, but this does not seem to have been the case. She then gave birth to Simeon and Levi: "This time my husband will become attached to me, because I have borne him three sons" (Genesis 29:32–34). She gives birth to a fourth son, named Judah.

Rachel, too, was sterile. Remarking that, prior to Yahweh's intervention, her sister was unable to give Jacob any offspring, Rachel flies into an argument with her husband. Let him give her children, or she'll die. Jacob answers, angrily: "Am I in the position of God, who has denied you motherhood?"(Genesis 30:2). So Rachel does the same as Sarah and puts her hand-maiden, Bilha, in Jacob's bed. And Bilha has two sons, sending Rachel into raptures: "God has done me justice; yes, he has heard my prayer and given me a son," she exclaims at the birth of the first, Dan. When her maidservant is confined with a second, she remarks: "I have fought a fateful battle with my sister, and I have won!" (Genesis 30:6–8).

But the "fateful battle" did not cease there. By the time she was unable to have children, in her turn Leah too imitated Sarah, and "took her slave girl Zilpah and gave her to Jacob as concubine," and she gave him two sons. Leah expresses her joy in the following words: "What blessedness! Women will call me blessed!" (Genesis 30:13). So in this case it is the opinion of women that counts the most.

What follows is even more surprising, in that it features the use of what the Bible dubs "apples of love," that is the mandrake, a plant whose Hebrew name has a common root with the word "love," and which was regarded as an aphrodisiac.

Leah's eldest son Reuben finds some in the fields at harvest time and brings them to his mother. Rachel also wants some, but Leah refuses: "Is it not enough to have taken my husband, without your taking my son's mandrakes as well?" (Genesis 30:15). But Rachel is no dupe and proposes a trade-off. In exchange for the "apples of love," the following night she will let Jacob sleep with his first wife once again. Leah accepts the offer, Yahweh offers his blessing, and once again Leah conceives, becoming pregnant on two subsequent occasions.

So, six boys in all. "God has given me a fine gift; now my husband will bring me presents, for I have borne him six sons" (Genesis 30:20). The seventh child was to be a girl, Dinah, whose life would be a miserable one, as she was raped by the son of a minor Canaanite despot. After this birth, Yahweh "remembered Rachel; he heard her and opened her womb" (Genesis 30:22). She had a son, Joseph, who was destined for a greater future (see p. 44–6).

Despite all their quarrels, the two sisters saw eye to eye on one point at least: they both harbored resentment against their father, Laban: "Does he not think of us as outsiders now? For not only has he sold us, but he has completely swallowed up the money he got for us"[9] (Genesis 31:15). So, when Yahweh told

Facing page
Giuliano Bugiardini,
The Rape of Dinah (detail), 1531,
Kunsthistorisches Museum, Vienna

Giambettino Cignaroli,
The Death of Rachel, 1769–70,
Galleria dell'Accademia, Venice

Jacob in a dream to return to the country of his father, they advised him to pay heed. He thus left with his wives, children, and a vast number of cattle taken from Laban. And Laban's fury could hardly have been appeased when he was told that Rachel had made off with some bronze or stone statuettes that her father kept in the home and which represented the "household gods" (Genesis 31:19).

Jacob's return to the country of his father was marked by a series of ordeals: the rape of Dinah first of all, followed by massacres perpetrated by her brothers to avenge it, and then by the death of Rachel. Pregnant once again, after great sufferings she gave birth to a son she scarcely had time to name Ben Oni ("son of my pain") before passing away. But Jacob preferred to call him Benjamin ("son of my right hand," or "son of good omen").

Rachel was to be venerated as one of the holy women who "built up the house of Israel" (Ruth 4:11). Her life, like that of her sister Leah and of other wives of the patriarchs, shows that Yahweh does not wait for humanity to become perfect before intervening in its history and forging alliances with it.

Fresh proof of this is given with Jacob, who expresses concern on the road back: how will his most fearsome enemy, his own brother Esau, react to his homecoming? Jacob starts by sending him messengers instructed to flatter and reassure, but they return in a panic, telling him that Esau is setting out to meet him with hundreds of armed men. What can he do? Jacob asks Yahweh: You chose me, so come to my aid. And Yahweh gives him an idea. This time, Jacob does not just send envoys: He piles them high with presents. One day, he offers a small herd, on the following day another. Altogether, he sends two hundred she-goats and twenty billy goats, two hundred ewes and twenty rams, she-camels, cows, bulls, she-asses, and asses. Yet even then he cannot be certain of obtaining the forgiveness and reconciliation he craves.

Then, one night, someone—an entity with the appearance of a man—starts a fight, wrestling with him until dawn. It is, according to the text, a real combat, a bout during which Jacob's hip is dislocated.

The patriarch understands that Yahweh is behind it all; Yahweh who, having overcome him, changes his name. As Abram had become Abraham, so Jacob becomes Israel. "No longer are you to be called Jacob, but Israel, since you have shown your strength against God and men and have prevailed." (Genesis 32:29). He is the one who, now he has grasped what it is to be holy, was ready to fight, perhaps hoping to pursue a life of trickery and compromise; but Yahweh, having seen him prepared to be reconciled with Esau, has dealt a decisive blow.

Henceforth Jacob will be a new man. His encounter with Esau was detached but peaceable. Before dying, Jacob gathers together all twelve of his sons—the majority hardly god-fearing men—who are to give rise to the twelve tribes of Israel and so transform a little clan (until then limited to the descendants of Abraham) into a great people.

Tamar

Though protected by Yahweh, the children of Jacob are far from perfect, as the story of Judah, Leah's fourth-born son, and his relationship with Tamar, his daughter-in-law proves. Judah was a moderate: he had interceded for Joseph, Rachel's first son, whom his brothers, jealous of old Jacob's penchant for him, were intent on eliminating. Joseph also irritated them by telling them about prophetic visions that betrayed his ambition. These men were not fainthearted.

Having thrown their brother into a—fortunately empty—cistern, Judah managed to dissuade them from their sinister plans, proposing that they rescue Joseph and sell him instead to a caravan of merchants making their way to Egypt.

Once this had been done, all the brothers, including Judah, told Jacob that Rachel's son had been attacked and devoured by a wild beast. Jacob lamented the loss of his son and eventually life returned to normal. Judah's affairs went well and his herd grew and grew and his vines produced plump grapes to whose juice he became partial. His father, who had seen him as a future leader, noted that his eyes were often "darkened with wine" (Genesis 49:12). Judah, however, left the clan to marry a Canaanite woman. A dim view was taken of this departure, because that region's customs were considered depraved and because it worshipped alien gods: as has already been said, Abraham had been afraid Jacob might marry a girl from that land.

Judah's wife gave him three sons. The eldest was called Er, and, when he came of age, he was married to a girl named Tamar, a pretty name meaning "palm tree," but a foreigner in the eyes of the clan of Jacob. Er died not long afterwards, because he had "offended Yahweh," as the Bible says, though it provides no further information (Genesis 38:7). Judah then applied the law known as "levirate." "Levi" means "brother-in-law," and the rule stated that if a husband died childless, his widow could be married to one of his brothers. As to die without issue was considered as dying twice over, it was hoped, through his brother, to give the deceased the child he had never had with his wife. It is possible that levirate had another, more materialistic purpose: the law ensured that the man's inheritance remained in the family.

Du pere ſamuel ſelon la bible et hyſtoire

Ns ipmis fu de raniathamꝛ ſa
phim du mont eſſraym qui
ot a nom delcana filz ierw
boam qui fu filz ielim qui
fu filz tan qui fu filz Sup
et fu delcana de la terre del
hiata ceſt adire de leſtlet

Judah, therefore, turned to his second son, Onan. "Take your brother's wife, and do your duty as her brother-in-law, to maintain your brother's line" (Genesis 38:8). Onan did indeed go to his brother's wife, but he did not play the game: every time he copulated with Tamar, he ensured his seed fell on the ground. Unwilling to provide his brother with progeny, he thus indulged in the practice that has perpetuated his name in the term "onanism." But Yahweh punished him, not so much for the act itself, as for disobeying the rule and, thus, Yahweh. Onan died soon afterward, to the great despair of Judah, and apparently of Tamar, too, as the sequel to the story shows.

Waiting for a third son, Shelah, to come of age and marry Tamar, Judah sent Tamar back to live with her family. Much time passed and still Tamar waited. Her mother-in-law, Judah's wife, then passed away. Tamar carried on waiting: the third son had attained adulthood, but he had not been offered to her as a husband.

One day, when Judah had completed the mourning rites, he went outside to shear his sheep. Tamar decided to use an artifice: removing her widow's weeds, she "wrapped a veil around her to disguise herself, and sat down … on the way" to a place of pilgrimage. "Judah, seeing her, took her for a prostitute, since her face was veiled. Going up to her on the road, he said, 'Here, let me sleep with you.' … 'What will you give me for sleeping with you?' she asked. 'I will send you a kid from the flock,' he said. 'Agreed, if you give me a pledge until you send it,' she replied." Judah asked what she had in mind: "Your seal and cord and the staff you are holding," she proposed. A deal then was struck; he followed her, and she became pregnant (Genesis 38:14–18). Some time later Judah decided to fulfill his promise, and he sent one of his friends to take the kid goat to Tamar, but the man could not find the prostitute. The locals, moreover, had never seen a woman at that place, and so, somewhat downcast, he returned home. Three months afterwards, some wagging tongue informed Judah that his daughter-in-law had strayed, worked as a prostitute, and become pregnant. Judah ordered her to be brought out and burned alive. He showed no mercy toward Tamar, though it should be recalled that for a man to have relations with a prostitute was no disgrace: the Law did not prohibit it.[10]

But Judah had forgotten about the articles he had left with Tamar as surety: telltale, personal belongings that would betray his identity. Tamar reminded him of them. He could only concede: "'She was right and I was wrong, since I did not give her to my son Shelah.' He had no further intercourse with her" (Genesis 38:26). If Judah "did not give her" to his son (in some translations, contrary to a time-honored practice, it is Shelah who is "given" to Tamar), it was because he had lost all confidence in the future, in life itself. Too bad for Tamar, he thought, too bad for Shelah. But in the end, life turned out the stronger.

Wool is gathered in spring and it was at shearing time that Judah was seized by his desire to have relations with a woman, even a prostitute. And if Tamar indulged in subterfuge, something the author of the text does not appear to condemn, it was in order to give life. She was confined with twins.

This narrative, an excursus in the cycle of Joseph's adventures after being sold into Egypt, provides a prime instance of the power of a woman's maternal drive: Tamar absolutely wants to have a child of the blood of her deceased husband. But the story has another meaning: the twins, Perez and Zerah, were the forefathers of two clans that go on to form the tribe of Judah, with Perez being David's ancestor. So it is that Tamar appears in the Jesus genealogy of St. Matthew's Gospel (Matthew 1:3), as if it were necessary to see, in her alien origin and in this dubious story, a portent of how the people of Yahweh were to open up to pagans.

The story of Hannah (Anne), mother of the prophet Samuel—more recent according to the account in the Bible—is also more traditional. Once again, as for the wives of the patriarchs, sterility plays a crucial role.

Hannah

Hannah, first wife of the somewhat shadowy Elkanah, was also unable to have issue. She suffered all the more from her predicament since a second wife, Peninnah, with a host of children, boys and girls, so many that the Bible does not even count them, was constantly vaunting her fertility. Yet, and this is relatively rare, Elkanah sympathized with Hannah's pain, doing his best to console her, giving her—for instance—twice the number of presents each time the family went on a pilgrimage: "Hannah, why are you crying? Why are you not eating anything? Why are you so sad? Am I not more to you than ten sons?" (1 Samuel 1:8). Such a remark is worth stressing since at this time sons counted more than anything else; though it is true that Peninnah had already given Elkanah his fair share.

Hannah, however, could draw little comfort from the attentions of her spouse. One day, when on a pilgrimage, after he has once again held forth, she starts weeping bitterly and makes a promise: if Yahweh gives her a boy, she will dedicate him to the Lord as a servant in the sanctuary. A priest passing through sees her lips "moving" in prayer and initially thinks she must be drunk. As she puts him right, she is told to "'Go in peace, and may the God of Israel grant what you have asked of him.' … With that, the woman went away; she began eating and was dejected no longer." Once back home, the following day, "Elkanah lay with his wife Hannah and Yahweh remembered her" (1 Samuel 1:11–20), and she gave birth to a boy whom she named Samuel. Once he was three years old and was weaned she fulfilled her promise and "led the child to Eli," handing Samuel over to the same priest who had thought she was inebriated. This boy grew into the prophet Samuel, considered by some as a new Moses, who received a series of divine revelations and introduced kingship to Israel.

As for Hannah, she composed a prayer praising Yahweh in these terms:

> My heart exults in Yahweh …
> The bow of the mighty has been broken
> but those who were tottering are now
> braced with strength …
> the hungry need labour no more
> (1 Samuel 2:1–5)

These verses announce, almost word for word, the *Magnificat* of the Virgin Mary: "My soul proclaims the greatness of the Lord … He has pulled down princes from their thrones and … filled the starving with good things" (Luke 1:46–53).

So it is that, over the centuries, from Sarah to Hannah and from Hannah to Mary, the mothers of Israel climbed mountains, accepted the incredible and accomplished the impossible, so as to shape their people and lead them onward, to God.

Heroines and protectors

Standing beside the bed, Judith murmured
to herself: "Lord God, to whom all strength belongs,
prosper what my hands are now to do for
the greater glory of Jerusalem; now is the time
to recover your heritage and to further my plans
to crush the enemies arrayed against us."
With that she went up to the bedpost by Holofernes'
head and took down his scimitar; coming closer
to the bed she caught him by the hair and said,
"Make me strong today, Lord God of Israel!"
Twice she struck at his neck with all her might,
and cut off his head.

(Judith 13:4–8)

Pages 52–53
Tintoretto, *Judith and Holophernes*
(detail), 1579,
Prado, Madrid

James Ensor, *The Discovery
of Moses* (or *Moses and the Birds*)
(detail), 1924, University of
California Art Museum, Berkeley

Heroines and protectors
Jochebed | Pharaoh's daughter | Zipporah | Naomi | Ruth | Rahab | Judith

His name is mentioned more than nine hundred times in the Bible. A giant of the faith. It was him the God of Israel chose to "go and tell the people all Yahweh's words and all the laws" (Exodus 24:3), but he is just as frequently presented as the person who wrote the Torah, the Law—or some parts of it, at least.

For Christians, he prepared the path for the Messiah, and was even present with Jesus at the Transfiguration (Matthew 17:1–6), clarifying and authenticating the shift from the Old to the New Covenant.

It was Moses, whose name derives from the Egyptian *mos*, meaning "he was born," or "newborn," but which can also be related to the Hebrew *mashah*, "to withdraw," because he was "drawn out of the water."

The story of the birth and rescue of the baby Moses demonstrates how he survived only thanks to three women: his mother and sister, of course, but also Pharaoh's daughter, an Egyptian woman whose name is not recorded by history. The Israelites, present in the land since the time of Joseph and Jacob, and initially greeted with open arms, had been condemned by her royal father to forced labor. For the immigrants had grown in number, built cities for Pharaoh, and farmed his lands. But now their "taskmasters" were making them work more and more, but without providing them with the materials necessary (Exodus 5:6–18). The Hebrews were inducing fear and had been threatened with out-and-out slavery.

Pharaoh said: "Look … the Israelites are now more numerous and more powerful than we are. We must take precautions to stop them from increasing any further or if war should break out, they might join the ranks of our enemies. They might take up arms against us and then escape from the country" (Exodus 1:9–10).

And so the people of the Covenant suffered. And Yahweh kept quiet, as if He had forgotten the promises He had made with Abraham, Isaac, and Jacob. For those who have faith in Him, God's silences, his apparent indifference to evil, are sometimes unbearable. But failing to see divine action, lacking absolute confidence in it, doesn't stop it existing.

For Yahweh had indeed already intervened on behalf of the Hebrews as they struggled under the Egyptian yoke. He had given them a leader, a guide the Lord would guide: Moses. The stress, however, is rarely laid on how he was saved by a female plot, and that, when he had to flee after killing an Egyptian who had abused a Hebrew, he was aided and abetted by another foreign woman, a Madianite, Zipporah.

Similarly, Ruth, a Moabite—and thus belonging to that same, much-maligned nation—had come with Yahweh and his people: she appears in the genealogy of Jesus (Matthew 1:5) as David's great-grandmother.

Rahab, too, a woman of Jericho and a prostitute, helped the Israelites, led by Joshua, to finally enter the Promised Land. While the beautiful and splendidly virtuous Judith saved the Hebrews by her faith in Yahweh and her heroism.

These women, and others too, of various origins, served as Yahweh's helpmeets, to assist and guide God's chosen people into the light, into freedom.

Pages 52–53
Nicolas Poussin, *The Exposition
of Moses*, c. 1624, Gemäldegalerie
Alte Meister, Dresden

First of all, of course, there was Moses' mother, Jochebed, daughter of the patriarch Levi, a descendant of Jacob and Leah. Levi had been a rough fellow, but his tribe soon specialized in the priesthood (the Levites). Already the mother of two children, Jochebed hid Moses for three months—as long as she could to save him from being killed.

Jochebed

And then there was a sister, Miriam, who is too often ignored. It was she whom Jochebed told to watch over the basket in which she had placed the newborn boy, close by the bank among the reeds. And, from her hiding place, she saw Pharaoh's daughter approach, accompanied by a small retinue.

Discovering the basket, the princess saw that the child was circumcised, and so a son of the Hebrews, and was filled with pity. Miriam, who did not lack courage, went up to the Egyptian girls and offered to go and find "among the Hebrew women" a wet nurse to feed the child. The princess approved and, naturally, Miriam hurried off to find Moses' own mother.

pharaoh's daughter

Miriam plays a consistent role in events. In the book of Micah, Yahweh reproaches his straying people and recalls all He has done for them: "My people, what have I done to you? How have I made you tired of me? Answer me! For I brought you up from Egypt, I ransomed you from the place of slave-labor, and sent you Moses, Aaron, and Miriam to lead you" (Micah 6:3–4).

zipporah

Here Moses' sister is placed almost on the same level as Moses, with her brother Aaron. The Bible lists her among the prophetesses (see p. 75–6), because, after leaving Egypt, it was she who led the dances and songs of the women to the sound of the tambourine (Exodus 15:20–21).

This woman prophet then had a strong character—and marked prejudices. She upbraided Moses for marrying a dark-skinned woman—in her eyes a foreigner, Zipporah—who had saved his life. Yahweh considered these reproaches serious enough to descend in a "column of cloud" and convene all three, Aaron, Moses, and Miriam. He severely reprimanded the young woman; by the time He left, she had acquired leprosy, and turned as white as a corpse. But Moses interceded for her, and her punishment was commuted to an exile of seven days outside the Israelite camp, which the people waited to elapse before proceeding on their march (Numbers 12:1–15).

Moses' plea to Yahweh was no more than Miriam deserved: after all, he owed her his life. As he did Pharaoh's daughter, who had taken him to the palace after his three years at the breast, who took care of his education and watched over him until manhood. Moses was a man saved by three women—not forgetting the princess's female entourage.

Subsequently, it was he who was to free his people from Pharaoh's shackles, though not without misgivings as to the enormity of his task: "Who am I to go to Pharaoh and bring the Israelites out of Egypt?" (Exodus 3:11).

In one form or another, the prophets were wont to express lassitude or their fear of being too weak, too lowly to fulfill the divine mission, but Yahweh answers them all: "I shall be with you" (Exodus 3:12).

If the tale of Miriam and the role she played deserves to be better known, the same can be said for the more involved story of Ruth. She was a Moabite. Towards the thirteenth century BCE, the Moabites had established themselves on the eastern shores of the Dead Sea, in what is today Jordan. It was a region

in which the majority of the population were nomads or seminomads.

They might farm for a time but they were mostly herders, though there were also craftsmen and merchants. They were sometimes rejected by other, more populous, better-armed, and better-organized tribes. And the gods, of course, played a significant role in these rivalries.

Belonging to the family of Abraham and descending from Lot's elder daughter, the Moabites had opposed the survivors of the Exodus led by Moses following the Covenant concluded with God in the Sinai.

The king of Moab, Balak, had even called in a famous soothsayer, Balaam, to lay a curse on the people of Israel in exchange for a generous hoard of gifts. Since the Jews had left Egypt and undertaken their exhausting, difficult, but in the end victorious march to the Promised Land, however, Yahweh's reputation had grown, and he was now feared even by outsiders like Balaam. Still, with one eye on the reward, the magus all the same decided to accede to the king's request.

He thus set off, with his two sons and the princes of Moab, to meet with Balak, mounted on a donkey—an honor at the time. The Bible has conferred a certain celebrity on this beast, because Yahweh, seeing the magician with such a large retinue, thought he should stop him in his tracks.

When the angel of Yahweh[1] bars Balaam's passage, the donkey understands and makes a detour through the fields. Balaam, though a soothsayer, has no inkling of what is going on and beats the animal to get it to return to the chosen route. Eventually they reach a sunken path, bending amid the vines, bordered by "a wall to the right and a wall to the left."

The donkey, seeing the angel waiting for the little caravan, scrapes against one of the walls, hurting Balaam's foot. Again he thrashes it. The angel, finally, stands in an even narrower place. This time, the donkey, which by now has had enough, lies down, only to receive a further barrage of blows.

Given the power of speech, it protests. At his wits' end, Balaam replies that if he had a sword, the donkey would already be dead. It meanwhile reminds its master of the good and faithful service it has rendered him over the years. Balaam finally grasps the situation, sees the angel of the Lord, and agrees to obey Him and Him alone. He thus goes to meet the king, but only to bless the Hebrews (Numbers 22:22–35).

Thus the Israelites can finally enter the country of Moab. But, where Balak and Balaam failed, the daughters of the land did better. Using other advantages, the women prostituted themselves, and soon the Hebrews were worshipping their gods. As a punishment, Moses, inspired by Yahweh, condemns twenty-four thousand warriors of Israel to die, but in the end God prevents the massacre (Numbers 25).

Moses dies shortly afterwards, but the curse laid on the Moabites persists: "No Ammonite or Moabite will be admitted to the assembly of Yahweh; not even his descendants to the tenth generation" (Deuteronomy 23:3).

And so Yahweh continues to write the history of His people in mysterious ways.

Thus, one day, when times were hard in an Israel riven by civil war, hunger forces an Israelite family to leave the little town borough of Bethlehem. This family settles in the land of Moab and the two sons marry the Moabites, Ruth and Orpah. In justifying this infraction of the edict, the rabbis, with subtle reasoning, allege that the rule excluded Moabite men, but not their women.[2] In all events, such subtleties did little to save the young bridegrooms, who, like their father, quickly died.

Naomi, mother-in-law of Ruth and Orpah, thus finds herself in the unenviable situation of being alone in a foreign land with two daughters-in-law. Once the famine ceases, she decides to set out

Pages 60–61
Sandro Botticelli, *The Story of Moses*
("The burning bush, "Moses kills
the Egyptian," "Moses protecting
the daughters of Jethro"), 1481–82,
Sistine Chapel, Vatican

Facing page
Ruth, after a miniature from
the *Bible de Sens*, fourteenth century,
Biblioteca Reale, Turin

again for Bethlehem, leaving her daughters-in-law who, she thinks, will be happier in their native land. But Ruth and refuses to desert her mother-in-law: Their shared misfortune seems to have brought them closer.

Naomi, however, insists that Ruth remain with the Moabites, since she does not have a son Ruth can marry in accordance with the law of the levirate (see p. 46). And even supposing that, back in Bethlehem, Naomi were to remarry (but "I am now too old," she observes), and even supposing she were to have sons, her daughters-in-law could hardly be expected to wait for them.

The situation is impossible! Full of bitterness, Naomi regrets advancing what are, after all, reasonable objections, but her two daughters-in-law dissolve into tears. Which way should she turn? At length Orpah decides to remain, but Ruth stands her ground and joins Naomi. But she cannot know how, as a Moabite, she will be received in Bethlehem. "Wherever you go, I shall go, wherever you live, I shall live," she says to Naomi. "Your people will be my people and your God will be my God" (Ruth 1:16).

Overcome by such a demonstration of affection, Naomi yields. Their arrival in Bethlehem creates uproar among the inhabitants, but apparently nobody takes against the Moabitess.

The two women have brought little with them and have trouble making ends meet. Then harvest time comes. Ruth sets off to glean, collecting the ears of wheat left by the reapers. The owner of the field, Boaz, a relative of Naomi's, appears: he is perfectly within his rights to drive Ruth, who has been busy since morning, out of the field. But in fact Boaz allows her to carry on, follow his "work-women" and "go to

naomi and ruth

the pitchers and drink what the servants have drawn," because he has forbidden the young men to "molest" her (Ruth 2:8–9). After she expresses astonishment at such kindness, he explains that he knows her story.

"May Yahweh repay you for what you have done and may you be richly rewarded by Yahweh, the God of Israel, under whose wings you have come for refuge" (Ruth 2:12). In Boaz's eyes, Ruth resembles Abraham. Like him, she has left everything to answer the call of the Lord. He even orders his servants to discreetly drop a few ears of corn from their sheaves so that she can pick them up.

By evening, Naomi has got wind of events. Feeling it is her "duty" to make her daughter-in-law "happily settled," she decides to play the matchmaker. Tonight, she tells Ruth, get up and "perfume [herself]" and go to Boaz after he has finished eating and drinking. When he gets ready for bed, make yourself a "place at his feet," and lie down and do what he tells you.

Naomi's intentions may be good, but it is a curious way of carrying on! Her hope is that Boaz, a little tipsy after a hard day in the fields, and not really knowing who the young woman is, will take Ruth and she will at last give her late husband issue.

Usually, it is the father-in-law who obtains a son for his daughter-in-law, with the same aim. This time it is the mother-in-law who takes on the role, together with a *goel*, a relative. But the guileless Ruth does not follow the script. She does wait until Boaz is asleep to go to him and lie down at his feet. When he awakes, surprised, he asks her who she is. But Ruth does not leave the initiative to him, as Naomi suggested. She invites him instead to take her under his protection and marry her. Praising her for wanting to perpetuate the line, Boaz nonetheless tells her in all honesty that there lives a member of Naomi's late

husband's immediate family who could easily take his place. Then, concerned for Ruth's reputation, he urges her to leave before dawn: on that night nothing more occurs between them.

This other relative having refused Ruth (for complicated reasons to do with an inheritance), Boaz eventually does marry Ruth and the "elders" of the neighborhood hail his decision: "May Yahweh make the woman about to enter your family like Rachel and Leah who together built up the house of Israel" (Ruth 4:11).

So it is that a foreigner, a scion of an enemy people, after so many trials and tribulations, takes her place among the founders of Israel. Ruth's fundamental role is confirmed, moreover, when she gives birth to a boy named Obed, who will become grandfather to Jesus' ancestor, King David.

Another foreigner figures in the genealogy of Jesus—and she is a prostitute. Named Rahab, she lived in Jericho, at the very gates of Jerusalem.

The chosen people had by then made it to the east bank of the Jordan. They were led by Moses' faithful companion Joshua, one of only two Hebrews[3] more than twenty years old who took part in the Exodus to enter the Promised Land, the others having perished in the desert or in battles during their forty years of wandering.

This grace was even refused to Moses, as he was not a warrior but a man with a direct relation to God: one had to be battle-hardened to enter the land of Canaan. Almost all the twelve scouts—one per tribe—sent by Moses to explore the country return in terror: the cities there, they report, are stoutly defended and inhabited by giants. Beside them, the Jews look like grasshoppers. Only Joshua and Caleb are of the opinion that, with the assistance of Yahweh, victory is possible.

But their advice is ignored and the people even think of setting out once again for Egypt, arousing the wrath of Yahweh, who is fed up with the Israelites' ceaseless complaining. Moses objects that, by punishing them, he would be discredited in the eyes of the Egyptians, so Yahweh forgives them, thus showing love to be the stronger (Numbers 14:20).

Moses then dies without ever entering the land of Canaan. Meanwhile Joshua joins together all the tribes of Israel to solemnly renew their commitment to the Covenant contracted in the Sinai, and soon they are ready to cross the River Jordan.

It is now that Yahweh offers spectacular assistance to His people. The first obstacle met by the Israelites is Jericho, on the other side of the river. Its well-defended fortifications seem of great concern to Joshua, who dispatches two spies to reconnoiter the area.

The two men go directly to Rahab, a prostitute. Did they know her already? Or had they deduced that her profession would make her a hospitable sort? The author of the story tells us nothing. Be that as it may, without hesitating, Rahab opens her door to them. But the inhabitants of Jericho are wary. They know something is afoot on the opposite bank of the river. And, in a city fearing imminent attack, the craziest rumors spread quickly. One of them, however, is true, and the king of Jericho is informed that two spies are in Rahab's house.

Knowing of her calling and her reputation, the king probably reckons that she is one of those rare townspeople who might let unknown individuals into her house without enquiring who they are and where they come from. He thus sends some henchmen to investigate: they are a bit brusque, as one might expect, but she tricks them.

She is clearly used to pulling the wool over people's eyes: if she were in the habit of giving away the identity

Rahab

of her customers, she would have gone out of business ages ago. She first hides the men "under some stalks of flax" covering the roof (Joshua 2:6). Then she comes over all innocent: two men she didn't know did indeed come to her but, as the gates of the city were shutting, they made off. And which way did they go? It was none of her concern. But the king's officers, rightly suspecting the presence of the Israelites, start their search near the Jordan.

In truth, Rahab was not guided solely by innate hospitality. Once the immediate danger has passed, she explains to the two spies that she knows why they are in the city: tongues often wag in establishments like hers. She is also aware that Yahweh has helped the Israelites cross several rivers before: for them the Jordan does not therefore present an insuperable obstacle. For reasons such as these, she has come to believe that their God, Yahweh, is the true God, in heaven as on earth.

She then pleads: she has just saved their lives. In exchange, let them swear before their God, who is also master of the world and of history, to protect her and her whole family and all that belongs to them, when the time comes. She ensures that she asks them for a sign that they will respect the vow—it's only fair.… The mark will be a scarlet thread that she will tie to her window as soon as the men make their escape. And they promise all she requests. She then tells them which paths they must take to avoid bumping into the king's constables and lowers them over the city walls in a basket.

The two spies keep their word and Joshua, now reassured, readies the people. As they make their way to the Jordan, now in full spate, the priests go before carrying the Ark of the Covenant. And, just as He had done at the time of the crossing of the Nile, Yahweh parts the waters. First the priests, then the people, traverse the dry riverbed.

Once in front of Jericho, Yahweh—the true commander in chief of this operation and of the conquest of the Holy Land—orders them to run every day round the city while seven priests blow ram's-horn trumpets.

On the seventh day, the people let out a great "war cry," and the city walls collapse, like a house of cards. Only the house of Rahab remains standing and she, together with her entire family, survives. Now, since she believed in the new world, she belongs to the people of Israel (Joshua 2; 6:1–25).

The evangelist Matthew cites the prostitute of Jericho as David's grandmother and therefore Jesus' third ascendant, since any person who adheres to the faith of Israel automatically forms part of its people. Early Christianity, in accepting the New Covenant with the pagans, was to adopt this rule as its own. Saint Cyprian, a great theologian and bishop of Carthage, who was to be beheaded by the Romans in the third century CE, sees Rahab as prefiguring the Church.

Judith was a very different woman, if the book devoted to her, which exalts her exploits, is to be believed.[4] The author of this book locates the episode at the time of Nebuchadnezzar, who was in fact the king of Babylon who invaded Palestine for the first time in 604 BCE; the book of Judith, however, has Nebuchadnezzar as a king of the Assyrians, though they were actually his enemies, and sets it in Nineveh, whereas in fact that city was destroyed by his father. The other main character in the narrative is a general named Holophernes, who lived about three centuries later. Obviously, our author was not overly concerned with either history or geography: he just wanted to tell the story of a heroine, basing it, perhaps, on real events more or less distorted as they were transmitted orally down the ages.

When he presented himself before Bethulia, a small village located in the highlands on the Jerusalem road, Holophernes was at the head of an immense army that had already conquered many nearby countries

Facing page
"Judith and Holophernes," illumination
from the *Vie des Femmes Célèbres*
by Antoine Dufour, c. 1505,
Musée Thomas Dobrée, Nantes

on behalf of his king (whoever he might have been). The Moabites and other enemies of Israel advised him not to risk the life of even one of his tens of thousands of soldiers by attacking Bethulia. The town was supplied from a spring that spouted from the foot of the hillside: it would be enough to turn off the water, encircle the city, and wait. Parched and soon famished, the inhabitants would end up dying or surrendering: if any of these mountain dwellers were foolhardy enough to defend themselves, they would pay dearly.

Finding this advice judicious, Holophernes acted accordingly. The plan almost succeeded. After a siege lasting thirty-four days, the population of the city, at the end of its tether and on the verge of rioting, demanded that its leaders capitulate. The headmen obtained a brief delay to think it over, probably hoping beyond hope for assistance from the Eternal, pleading with him over the following five days to extricate them from their predicament.

It is at this juncture that Judith intervenes.

She was "very beautiful and charming to see" (Judith 8:7). She was also very wealthy, but, as a widow, she lived an ascetic life and "feared God."

She thus convenes all the heads of the city, saying, in substance: You just don't understand. You can't issue the Almighty with ultimatums, like you do with a man. But if you deliver up the city, all Judaea will be taken and our holy shrines will be pillaged.

But their only answer is to entreat her to ask the Lord "to send us a downpour to fill our storage wells" (Judith 8:31). Judith now realizes that these so-called leaders are frankly useless.

She will have to act herself and alone. Let them open the gates of the city for her, at night, and she will leave with her maidservant: giving no details as to what she is going to do, she just asks them to keep their

mouths shut. Instead—and rather immodestly, though perhaps under divine inspiration—she declares: "I intend to do something the memory of which will be handed down to the children of our race from age to age" (Judith 8:32).

judith

The men obey. She starts by praying, face to the ground, pouring ash over her head. Her plea to Yahweh—written down subsequently obviously, since it reveals part of her plan—is a beautiful prayer, made on behalf of the poor and the oppressed, summarized in the final verses:

> Observe their arrogance, send your fury on their heads, give the strength I have in mind to this widow's hand. By guile of my lips strike down slave with master, and master with retainer. Break their pride by a woman's hand. Your strength does not lie in numbers, nor your might in strong men; since you are the God of the humble, the help of the oppressed, the support of the weak, the refuge of the forsaken, the Saviour of the despairing. Please, please, God of my father, God of the heritage of Israel, master of heaven and earth, creator of the waters, king of your whole creation, hear my prayer. Give me a beguiling tongue to wound and kill those who have formed such cruel designs against your covenant, against your holy dwelling place, against Mount Zion, against the house belonging to your sons. And demonstrate to every nation, every tribe, that you are the Lord, God of all power, all might, and that the race of Israel has no protector but you. (Judith 9:10–14).

Having thus prayed, she "removed the sackcloth she was wearing and, taking off her widow's dress … put on the robe of joy" and "anointed herself plentifully with perfume." Tying a turban round her head, she draped

Facing page
Massimo Stanzione, *Judith with the Head of Holophernes*, c. 1630–35, The Metropolitan Museum of Art, New York

herself in jewelry and, in short, "made herself beautiful enough to beguile the eye of any man who saw her" (Judith 10:3–4). Even the men of her own camp were not immune. Prayer was now to be replaced by trickery.

So Judith sets out, accompanied by her handmaid, and soon encounters an advanced party of Assyrians. She asks to be taken to their chief, offering to show them, she says, the best way to take the city without bloodshed. The soldiers readily put their trust in such an imposing and alluring woman. The junior officer in charge of the post even offers her an escort to take her to Holophernes' camp. Our author, no more modest than Judith herself, uses this as a pretext to sing the praises of Israel once again. In the camp, he writes, "they were immediately impressed by her beauty" and admired the Israelites for having such specimens among them. "'Who could despise a people who have women like this?' they wondered" (Judith 10:19).

Judith thus meets Holophernes, whose tent is adorned with gold, emeralds, and precious stones. The author places great stress on the grandeur of the scene. And Judith, not averse to flattery in her cause, even cries: "Long life to Nebuchadnezzar!" But she doesn't spare the sins of her fellow citizens either: they are guilty and must be punished, while she, a pious woman, will pray to her God to ask Him for the most opportune moment to take the city.

Holophernes is completely besotted. His rapture knows no bounds and he answers: "Your God shall be my God!" (Judith 11:23). Judith, who at first sight enflames the desire of the enemy chief, remains in the camp, where she is feted by all, for three days. He ends up inviting her to a great banquet that finishes in predictable fashion.

All the guests are requested to leave the tent and Judith and Holophernes remain alone. But he has "collapsed wine-sodden on his bed" (Judith 13:2). At once, the woman seizes his scimitar, calls on Yahweh and, twice, strikes him at the base of the neck, slicing off the general's head. Handing it to her maidservant, who puts in a sack, she walks out of the camp (as she often did to pray) and returns to her people, taking care to reassure them that nothing untoward took place while she was with the now defunct enemy chief.

Holophernes's head is impaled on the summit of the ramparts. Seeing their chief is no more, the terrorized Assyrians take flight. The soldiers of Bethulia pursue them, eventually helped by others from Jerusalem. Of course, they plunder the enemy camp—such are the ways of war. After a sack lasting thirty days, the victors then set off on a pilgrimage to Jerusalem to offer part of the spoils to the Temple.

Three months later, Judith returns to Bethulia. Rejecting every offer of marriage, she lives for a hundred and five years. "Never again during the lifetime of Judith, nor indeed for a long time after her death, did anyone trouble the Israelites" (Judith 16:25).

Thus did a woman, beautiful and intelligent, succeed in derailing the machinery of death. "Because the Lord," says the Bible, "is a God who breaks the battle-lines" (Judith 16:2). Judith, a woman of prayer, made herself His instrument.

Although she deploys trickery and lies, it is true, it is only to show the inhabitants of Bethulia and of Jerusalem that faith alone can save the Jewish people. In the book dedicated to her, which reads like one long parable, it is significant that "Judith" in Hebrew means, simply, Jewess.

the prophetesses

There was a prophetess, too, Anna the daughter of Phanuel, of the tribe of Asher. She was well on in years. Her days of girlhood over, she had been married for seven years before becoming a widow. She was now eighty-four years old and never left the Temple, serving God night and day with fasting and prayer. She came up just at that moment and began to praise God; and she spoke of the child to all who looked forward to the deliverance of Jerusalem.

(Luke 2:36–38)

Pages 72–73
"The Presentation at the Temple,"
illumination from the *Psautier de Mélisande*,
c. 1131–43, British Library, London

Rembrandt, *Anna the Prophetess*
(or *The Artist's Mother*) (detail), 1631,
Rijksmuseum, Amsterdam

The prophetesses
Miriam | Deborah | Jael | Huldah | Anna

"Prophetess." Neither the word nor the quality it represents appear often in the Bible.

Obviously, a prophet is above all a man who transmits the word, even the orders, of a higher authority. The prophet speaks in the name of Yahweh; he is His mouthpiece. He cannot just appoint himself a prophet. It is Yahweh who gives him his function, who allots him his status.

Jeremiah, considered as one of the greatest prophets, explains how he was predestined before he was "formed in the womb," and was "appointed…as prophet to the nations" before he was born (Jeremiah 1:4–5). Yahweh explains his role thus: "'Say whatever I command you. … There! I have placed my words into your mouth'" (Jeremiah 1:7–9). So, as circumstances dictate, the prophets gradually reveal the intentions of Yahweh and the plans he has in mind for His people and for all humanity.[1]

Bible specialists usually reserve the term "prophet" for a limited number of men divided into four "major" and twelve "minor," or "later," prophets. For Christians, Jesus is, as the evangelist John writes, "him of whom Moses in the Law and the prophets wrote" (John 1:45).

Although prophecy seems the preserve of men, little by little the tradition admitted the existence of female equivalents. Thus, a text in the Talmud considers that God sent to Israel forty-eight prophets and seven prophetesses. In fact, it is no easy task to find them in the Bible, and the women are much less well known. It is true, as Josy Eisenberg[2] has underlined, that they "did not leave a major literary corpus behind them." It is equally possible that some of their words have been lost over time.

The first to earn the name of prophetess in the Bible was Miriam, Moses' elder sister who, in the attempt to save her baby brother, was brave enough to address Pharaoh's daughter (see p. 56).

But there were others, no less courageous. In particular at the time of the "Judges," which was a very tough period for the chosen people.

The Israelites called "judges" did not operate—or did not only operate—in the area of justice. The Hebrew word is closer to "head, chief" and the Bible sometimes calls them "saviors." They are men who did all they could to save their clan or tribe from some immediate danger or to face down the occasional enemy. Such adversaries often loomed when Israel had sinned and become beguiled by the gods of neighboring peoples. In His fury, Yahweh would then abandon His people to their fate (when they would be pillaged, for example). But as He at least remained faithful to the covenant, He would send down a "judge" to put them back on the straight and narrow. Unfortunately, when such judges suddenly passed away, the people would start again, emboldened to sin "even more than their ancestors" (Judges 2:12–19).

The first two "judges" were called Othniel and Ehud; but the third was a woman, Deborah. She rewards examination—as do the much-neglected Huldah, and Anna, well known among the Christians, the fourth woman to whom the Bible grants the title "prophetess."

As we have seen, the prophet Micah, a contemporary of the great Isaiah, placed Miriam almost on a par with Moses (see p. 56).

According to legend, when the Hebrews were dying of thirst in the Sinai Desert, it was she who found a well. Whether or not she is dubbed a "prophetess," she was clearly an exceptional individual.

After Jericho had been captured, the chosen people settled in Canaan, where the Israelites had not always been particularly welcome. After Joshua died without a successor, war broke out. The Israelite tribes settled in various territories, trying to survive as best they could, every man for himself. But the Canaanites were still there, sometimes soft-soaping to convince the Hebrews to adore their gods, but in general openly hostile. What is more, they were more united than ever under the aegis of Jabin, who ruled in Hazor[3]—a city destroyed by Joshua—and had at their disposal an army with "nine hundred iron chariots" under the command of a certain Sisera.

For some twenty years, Jabin harried the Israelites, before the prophetess Deborah intervened. Unlike many other "judges," Deborah, seated beneath a palm tree up in the mountains, actually dispensed justice. People would go to consult her, listen to her advice, resolve disputes, or assert their rights. But, so hard-pressed were they by the despot Jabin, that they could only reach her by taking a long detour. They ended up pleading their cause with Yahweh and begging Him to save them. And Yahweh replied through the words of Deborah.

Miriam

deborah

She summoned a certain Barak and called upon him to gather together ten thousand men belonging to two tribes, that of Zebulun and that of Naphtali, descendants of Jacob. Barak began by being reticent. Admittedly, she was only conveying a promise that Yahweh had just made to her: "I shall entice Sisera, the commander of Jabin's army … with his tanks and his troops; and I shall put him in your power" (Judges 4:7). Still, he had to weigh up the risks. And why had Yahweh chosen a woman to announce his victory to him? To make sure, she should accompany him: "If you come with me, I shall go; if you will not come, I shall not go." Deborah decides to follow him, though not without first pointing out that, under such conditions, "the glory will not be [his] for Yahweh will deliver Sisera into the hands of a woman" (Judges 4:6–9).

So they climbed Mount Tabor together, accompanied by ten thousand men. Sisera was soon informed. At the head of his contingent of chariots, he went on the attack against the Israelites, who had undone their hair (a ritual of holy war when they consecrated themselves to Yahweh).

Although far inferior in numbers, the Israelites carried the day easily. Yahweh struck the Canaanites with panic, while their general, Sisera, clambering out of his tank, fled on foot: Barak's army gave no quarter and every last man was put to the sword.

Sisera hoped to find refuge with an ally of his king called Heber the Kenite. This man's wife, Jael, left her tent as soon as she saw him coming and enjoined

Palma Giovane, *The Death of Sisera*,
Musée des Beaux-Arts Thomas Henry,
Cherbourg

Facing page
Francesco Solimena, *Deborah and Barak*,
c. 1731, Graf Harrach'sche
Familiensammlung, Rohrau

Facing page
Salomon de Bray, *Jael*, *Deborah*, *and Barak*, 1635, Museum
Catharijneconvent, Utrecht

him to accept hospitality, hiding him beneath a rug. When he begged for water, like a mother she gave him milk instead, until, exhausted, he fell asleep.

What happened next is horrendous. Jael "took a tent-peg and picked up a mallet; she crept up softly to him and drove the peg into his temple right through to the ground … and so he died" (Judges 4:21).

The narrative of this battle and the commander's death is accompanied, in the book of Judges, by a "Song of Deborah and Barak," a victory chant celebrating Yahweh in His fight against the enemies of His people who are also His enemies. The Song also hails Jael: "of the tent-dwelling women, may she be the most blessed!" The long wait of the defeated general's mother is also described: "At the window, she leans and watches, Sisera's mother, through the lattice, 'Why is his chariot so long coming? Why so delayed the hoof-beats from his chariot?' Jael The wisest of her ladies answers, and she to herself repeats, 'Are they not collecting and sharing out the spoils: a girl, two girls for each warrior; a booty of colored and embroidered stuff for Sisera, one scarf, two embroidered scarves for me?'" (Judges 5:28–30).

The anguish of the mother is combined with the evocation of the prisoners of war, young girls shared out between the soldiers, delivered up to their pleasure. And yet Jael is lauded for her murderous deceit: it is at once shocking and revealing.

For in such wars, women could only bandage wounds, wait in fear for the return of their warriors (taking solace perhaps in the idea of the spoils—other women and their adornments), or bewail the dead.

But two of them were given, or took on for themselves, quite another role.

First Jael, in whom Sisera trusted. Because he was a chief, because she was a woman, and because he could not imagine that she felt anything for the women whom he would simply share out among his soldiers. He orders her about as he would a sentinel: "'Stand at the tent door'" (Judges 4:20), never thinking for a moment that she might act on her own initiative.

As for Deborah, she had to go with the incredulous and timorous Barak so he would believe what she said—that is, the word of Yahweh, which she was conveying to him. In this way he was humiliated: Sisera slipped through his fingers; clearly, right was not on his side. Victory over the brutal enemies of Israel was thus won with the aid of two supposedly feeble females.

Faced by such material today, readers may feel qualms. This shows a lack of awareness of what war means, though. It is also to forget that the age of the judges was a time when the Covenant and the Law were being flouted and that the purpose of the Bible— its books constituting the national library of the Hebrews—is in fact pedagogic. For over the centuries, the chosen people often fell short of the ideal; and the prophets' role was to tell them so, repeatedly.

The Yahweh of the age of the judges remains faithful to his people, but threatens them when they stray. And this situation lasts for century after century, as the story of another prophetess attests, the virtually forgotten Huldah.

This time, again, the elect find themselves divided. The book of Judges ends with this disillusioned observation: "The Israelites then dispersed, each man to rejoin his tribe and clan, each leaving that place to his own heritage. In those days, there was no king in Israel and everyone did as he saw fit" (Judges 21, 24–25).

And then the day came that the great prophet Samuel—the son of Hannah the infertile (see p. 50), whom many would now come to consult— received Saul, a "handsome man in the prime of life" (1 Samuel 9:2), who had a problem: he couldn't

find his father's straying donkeys. Finally, they are discovered. And Samuel throws a banquet in his honor. Saul's astonishment knows no bounds on the following day when Samuel pours a vial of oil over his head and announces that Yahweh has chosen him as "leader of His people Israel" (in another version, he is chosen by lot).

Once king, Saul wins great victories over the Philistines, who were at that time oppressing the Israelites. But sometimes even he disobeys Yahweh. Samuel, though he has a great fondness for Saul, is forced to aver that he is no longer worthy of being king.

His successor, David, was to be just as famous. He settled in Hebron, some forty kilometers from Jerusalem, where he exercised his kingship. However, at that time, one of Saul's sons was crowned monarch of the Transjordan and Northern Israel, so that there were two kingdoms, one in the South and the other in the North. David, crowned king of the South, the kingdom of Judah, and then, at the request of the local tribes, of the North, finally unified the country.

Following the reign of his son Solomon, however, the peoples of the North once again seceded.

The tribe of Judah remained faithful to the house of David and, to a certain extent, to Yahweh—though such fidelity was limited, since throughout the eighth century the kingdom of the South was ruled by impious and idolatrous kings.

Disorder became the norm: in 640 BCE King Amon, who did all that "displeases Yahweh" (2 Kings 21:20), was assassinated by his servants. The people unseated them in their turn and put the king's eight-year-old son, Josias, on the throne. Henceforth, things were to change, because Josias wanted to be faithful to the God of David, his grandfather, whose path he intended to follow "not deviating from it to right or left" (2 Kings 22:2). In particular, the king embarked on repairs to the Temple of Jerusalem with some surprising consequences.

The high priest, the master of the Temple, announces to the king's secretary that in the building he has found the Book of the Law, the Torah.

Paolo Veronese, *The Crowning of David*, c. 1555–60, Kunsthistorisches Museum, Vienna.

This raises the question: how is it possible that the Law of Moses had been ignored by a young king so anxious to return to the God of King David? When, however, the king has its contents read aloud to him by his secretary, he is astonished and rends his clothes, fearing the worst: the predictions ascribed to Moses include a host of catastrophic punishments for this wayward people. Josias wants to get to the bottom of the matter and constitutes a delegation led by the high priest to "consult Yahweh on behalf of me" (2 Kings 22:13).

"Consulting Yahweh" was not rare in those days: prophets too were often questioned. What was exceptional, however, was that Josias' delegates went off to confer with a woman, Huldah, even though several prophets were living at the time in Jerusalem—to start with, one of the greatest, Jeremiah, who perhaps did not enjoy much consideration at this juncture.

The author (or authors) of the second book of Kings himself appears so surprised by this story that he hastens to provide the woman's address and pedigree of her husband, whose grandfather had been "keeper of the wardrobe [vestments]" at the Temple.

Huldah's pronouncements do little to reassure the king's envoys: "Yahweh … says this: 'I am going to bring disaster on this place and the people who live in it—all the words of the book read by the king of Judah. Because they have abandoned me and sacrificed to other gods, so as to provoke my anger by their every action, my wrath is kindled against this place, and nothing can stop it'" (2 Kings 22:16–17). However, she adds a word of compassion for the king himself: "Because you have torn your clothes and wept before me, I too have heard—Yahweh says this. So look, when I gather you to your ancestors, you will be gathered in your graves in peace, you will not live to see the great disaster I am going to bring on this place" (2 Kings 22:19–20).

Having received this message, Josias gathers all the inhabitants of Jerusalem in the Temple, "the whole populace, high to low" (2 Kings 23:2), reads them the book and renews the Covenant.

Huldah

Giotto, *The Presentation of Jesus at the Temple* (detail), c. 1303–10, Cappella degli Scrovegni, Padua

Facing page
Giovanni di Paolo, *The Presentation at the Temple*, 1449, Pinacoteca Nazionale, Siena

This king, to whom the prophetess had promised a peaceful death, was in fact killed during a battle against the Egyptian pharaoh, Neko. In the meantime, he was to smash many idols and altars devoted to the pagan deities.

Apart from these few verses, the Bible never mentions Huldah again.[4]

The next woman it endows with the title of prophetess, Anna, who belongs to the New Testament of the Christians, is hardly described at greater length.

Like Huldah, Anna is a woman of prayer and prediction. The only evangelist to refer to her, Luke, was, according to several second-century authors, a Syrian from Antioch and a physician. A talented writer with a penchant for reasoning, his intention was to demonstrate how, from the origin of Israel, through the all-important event **Anna** of Jesus' life, and on to the Church, it is the same plan of Yahweh-God that is being realized.

And in this plan, Jerusalem fulfills a central role: it is then hardly surprising that Luke recounts the rite of the purification at the Temple and refers to an old lady named Anna.

For all mothers, purification was an obligation: for forty days after birth, a young woman was regarded as impure (see p. 22).

Mary subjects herself to this obligation; as—and this is more surprising (since Luke writes: "their purification")—does Joseph. They thus enter the Temple of Jerusalem located on the opposite side of the city from Herod's palace. They first come across an elder called Simeon, "an upright and devout man." "It had been revealed to him by the Holy Spirit that he would not see death until he had set eyes on the Christ of the Lord" (Luke 2:26). The young couple puts the child in his arms, and Simeon prophesies: "Look," he says to Mary, "he is destined for the fall and for the rise of many in Israel … and a sword will pierce your soul too" (Luke 2:34–35).

A very venerable lady then crosses the young couple's path: Anna. Luke, though more interested in Simeon, provides further particulars: she is eighty-four years old, was married for seven years and never remarried, her father was called Phanuel (meaning "face of God") and she belonged to the tribe of Asher (son of Jacob and Zilpah, Leah's maidservant) who had established themselves on the shores of the Mediterranean, in a relatively prosperous region.

Anna spent practically every day at the Temple, in prayer and fasting. Unlike Simeon, the prophetess did not speak to the young couple, but, having seen them, "she began to praise God; and she spoke of the child to all who looked forward to the deliverance of Jerusalem" (Luke 2:38)—the city predestined for the Messiah's task of salvation.

In the Bible the forename Anna seems especially prevalent among pious women, one example being the mother of the prophet Samuel. The New Testament prophetess, whom the evangelist does not quote, confines her message to the people.

the queens

*It happened towards evening when David
had got up from resting and was strolling
on the palace roof, that from the roof he saw
a woman bathing; the woman was very beautiful.
David made enquiries about this woman and
was told, "Why, that is Bathsheba, daughter
of Eliam and wife of Uriah the Hittite." David
then sent messengers to fetch her. She came
to him, and he lay with her, just after she had
purified herself from her period. She then went
home again. The woman conceived and sent
word to David, "I am pregnant."*
(2 Samuel 11:2–5)

Pages 86–87
Jan Massys, *David and Bathsheba*
(detail), 1562, Musée du Louvre, Paris

Konrad Witz, *The Queen of Sheba*
before King Solomon (detail),
c. 1435–37, Gemäldegalerie, Berlin

the queens

Bathsheba | The queen of Sheba | Jezabel | Athaliah | Esther

The fate of the Ark of Covenant, which had already allowed the Hebrews to cross the Jordan without getting their feet wet, provides a depressing indicator of Israel's decadence. The Ark had been set up at Silo in the north of the country, where the great prophet Samuel spent his early years. But a great danger hung over this divided country: attacks from the Philistines.

They came from the shores of the Aegean Sea and Anatolia, and had initially attempted to settle in the Nile Delta. The pharaoh, Ramses III had, however, driven back them toward the coast at the foot of the mountains of Canaan, to the side of Gaza in particular. Harassed on the coast, the Philistines dreamed of penetrating into the hinterland.

They at first won several battles, to the point that the Israelites decided to go to Silo to fetch the Ark, so that its miraculous power might repel their enemies. This idea, however, proved a disaster: though the Philistines were impressed by the Ark, they returned to the fray and, to crown it all, made off with it, setting it up in the sanctuary of a god of their own named Dagon.

This time, Yahweh got angry: the statue of Dagon was broken into a thousand pieces, and a fatal disease struck the inhabitants, who lost no time in sending the Ark on to their neighbors. After they were smitten by another scourge, they too offloaded it, and so it continued. In the end, the Philistines placed the Ark on a cart drawn by two cows which pulled it to the nearest Israelite territory. Overjoyed, of course, the inhabitants nevertheless did not observe all the necessary rituals, and soon they were beset by further tribulations.

The Ark was transferred to a neighboring town until the day when King David came to search it out.

Such external dangers made the Israelites realize that they had to unite to survive. They demanded a king. Samuel was not wholly convinced since, to his mind, only Yahweh could truly gather the people together. The Israelites, however, would not back down. If other peoples have kings, why shouldn't they? Samuel ended up ceding the point—in one version with inspiration from Yahweh—and Saul became the first king (see p. 82). His realm soon split into two, though: one to the north, the other to the south, and the only kings to enter the annals of history were David and Solomon.

Now we come to the question of the place of women in the lives of these rulers.

David had two successive queens: Michal, Saul's younger daughter, who played a minor role, and Bathsheba. As for Solomon, in what was a sign of the times, he married Pharaoh's daughter. The first book of Kings reports that he adored Yahweh but that he also "loved many foreign women" (1 Kings 11:1), the foremost of whom was—as legend has it—the queen of Sheba. As for Joram, a sovereign of the kingdom of the South, and not a household name, he espoused the far more celebrated Athaliah.

But finally a Jewess was to become queen, though not over her own people: Esther. Apart from her, the wives of the kings recorded in the Bible seem to have shared a common trait: they participated in power, and were not above using trickery and intrigue.

As Deuteronomy—the book of the Bible that outlines and codifies the Law, the Torah—had already stated (in reference to the rules imposed in Israel on entering the Promised Land): future kings should not have too many wives lest this "lead their heart astray" (Deuteronomy 17:17). However, this was a recommendation the majority were prepared to ignore. In addition, after due deliberation, the rabbis conceded that a king could have eighteen wives! This finding was based on a remark made by the prophet Nathan to King David. In order to marry Bathsheba, David killed her husband, one of his officers called Uriah the Hittite, with a subterfuge. For which Nathan, speaking explicitly in the name of the Lord, reproaches him vigorously. All the more so, God added using the prophet's mouth, since "I gave … your master's wives into your arms" and "if this is too little, I will add as many again and as many again" (2 Samuel 12:8).[1] The rabbis counted that David already had six wives. Twice "as many again" makes twelve, a figure added to the first six, giving a total of eighteen.

The story of how David met Bathsheba is well known. That year the king had not accompanied his army in the war against the Ammonites, an Aramaean tribe living north of the Dead Sea. One evening, strolling about his palace terrace, he saw a very attractive woman bathing some way off.

Beguiled, the king asked his servants who she was, and one answered: "Why! that is Bathsheba, daughter of Eliam and wife of Uriah the Hittite" (2 Samuel 11:3). This "Why!" is revealing: how could the king have been unaware of such a beauty only a stone's throw away from his palace and, what is more, the wife of one of his officers (though a foreign mercenary, admittedly)?

Bathsheba

He desired her. He was king. She was a subject and had just performed her ablutions after her menses. He ordered her to be fetched and "lay with her" (2 Samuel 11:4). Then she returned home. Later noticing she had become pregnant, she promptly alerted David.

Bathsheba's enemies (and her rise meant she had many), and countless other commentators in their wake, have been of the opinion that she calculated the whole affair: taking a bath, naked, on a terrace; accepting the king's invitation without objection, all the while aware that, her period of "impurity" having ended, she was liable to be fertile: all very suspicious. As Uriah, in particular, was to observe.

On the pretext of needing news of the army, David summons him and then orders him to return home. Uriah is having none of it and provocatively decides to sleep at the door of the palace with the guards. This comes to the attention of David, though, who asks him why he is camped in front of the palace.

Uriah replies that, unlike his companions in arms, he doesn't feel like going out drinking or sleeping with his wife. David insists and gets him drunk: His intention is that once the soldier has bedded his wife, he will be under the impression he is father of David's child. But Uriah digs his heels in and spends the night with the sentinels.

The next day, David orders him to take a letter to the commander of the army, Joab, asking him to expose Uriah "where the fighting is fiercest and then fall back so he gets wounded and is killed" (2 Samuel 11:15). Joab obeys and Uriah loses his life in battle. This is not an unusual practice in war: it is easy to arrange the death of someone from one's own camp who has fallen out of favor or committed a misdeed.

Uriah is not the only to lose his life, though. Other warriors, among them a high-ranking officer, also fall. When David learns of it, he feigns anger. But Joab is not overly concerned: he could have no doubt as to the purpose of the operation.

The author of the story says much that blackens David's name, while Uriah is described as a loyal soldier as well as a good comrade.

Hence the anger of Yahweh, who sends Nathan to threaten the king and foretell that David's wives will be taken from him and violated before his very eyes and that the child to whom Bathsheba (now, after the requisite period of mourning, the king's wife) has just given birth will die.

Though David fasts, spends the night on the bare ground, refusing all sustenance, the prediction comes to pass: on the seventh day, the child dies.

The Bible, which long accepted polygamy, condemns adultery—which was seen as something very different, obviously. And to adultery, David added assassination, so Yahweh cannot spare him; the death of Bathsheba's firstborn is followed by that of two of David's sons; the eldest boy, Amnon, rapes his sister and is in consequence murdered by his brother, Absalom, who then takes over their father's harem, since he is by now very old.

Absalom is later slaughtered by a gang faithful to the king, even though David had made it known that his son was to be saved. A sorry end indeed for the reign.

But long before this, Bathsheba had paved the way. She had had a second son by David, to whom she gave the name of Solomon. He was not even David's eldest, since the king had already had several wives by the time she knew him. There was, for instance, a certain Adonias, who played the heir apparent at court and in the streets of Jerusalem, rallying the notables to his cause and making enemies, while the old king let him do his worst.

Adonias, it seems, was not especially bright: one day, for a feast at which sheep, oxen, and fatted calves were to be slaughtered, he invites the entire court—save for Solomon and the prophet, Nathan. This time, Nathan takes Bathsheba's side—and he was some ally to have.

He devises a scheme: she should go and see her old husband and remind him of an oath (one nobody had in fact ever heard), according to which Solomon should become king. And she should also make her husband understand that if ever Adonias was to reign, her life and that of her son would be in danger.

While Bathsheba goes to the king to put this cunning plan into action, Nathan turns up, as if by chance. All innocence, he reveals that he has just discovered Adonias's claims to the throne! David now pays heed and designates Solomon. The people "escort[ed] him back, with pipes playing and loud rejoicing and shouts to split the earth" (1 Kings 1:40).

Adonias at once loses his allies: all he can do now is to throw himself on Solomon's mercy. Solomon promises him that his life is safe, instructing him to "Go to your house" (1 Kings 1:53).

The next episode in this convoluted story is ambiguous. Rather than keeping out of trouble, and though he could hardly be unaware that she is unlikely to be impartial, Adonias goes to Bathsheba. He has a serious request for her: he wishes to marry a young virgin named Abishag, who had given comfort to the old David, lying by his side without the king "knowing" her.

Bathsheba agrees to speak to Solomon about it. Can't she see that to take the wife of a preceding king means coveting his throne, too? Or does she think the rule does not apply as David did not "know" the gorgeous Abishag? (Of course in the Bible, "knowing" a woman meant having sexual relations with her.) Solomon, on the other hand, does not hesitate. Seeing this as a new ploy in Adonias's bid for the kingdom, he has him put to death, together with several other suspects. The author of the Bible story notes without further ado: "And now the kingdom was securely in Solomon's hand" (1 Kings 2:46).

Bathsheba seems pleased enough; in conveying Adonias's request, perhaps she was trying to engineer the death of someone who represented a potential danger for her son. That is the opinion of the relatively numerous commentators who regard her as a schemer. And the evangelist Matthew is perhaps of their number: in composing the genealogy of Jesus, in which Solomon's mother necessarily features, he designates her simply as "the wife of Uriah" (Matthew 1:6).

Solomon's wives, numerous and often foreign, do not seem to have played a significant role in his life. The king initially married the daughter of a Pharaoh (perhaps Psusennes II), for reasons—one might say today—of foreign policy.

Solomon's women included Moabites, Ammonites, and others, all belonging to peoples of whom Yahweh had told the Israelites: "You are not to be among them nor they among you, or they will surely sway your hearts to their own gods" (1 Kings 11:2). As indeed came to pass.

In the Bible, Solomon has seven hundred wives of princely rank, and three hundred concubines, and even worshipped some of their gods. Displeasing Yahweh, he was told that he would have his kingdom taken from him, though one tribe would be left to his son, destined to become the kingdom of the South, that of Judah, whose king was Roboam, son of Naama, an Ammonite.[2]

Neither Pharaoh's daughter nor Naama played any great role in Solomon's life, and history and legend have preferred another queen: the famous queen of Sheba.

Although she has been the source of a thousand novels and tall tales, not even her real name has come down to us. A Muslim legend calls her Balkis, but Ethiopia mentions Makedo. The Bible says simply: "The queen of Sheba heard of Solomon's fame and came to test him with difficult questions" (1 Kings 10:1).

She arrived in Jerusalem at the head of a caravan of camels laden with all the riches of Arabia. It was said that at that time the kingdom of Sheba (currently Yemen) had become prosperous by trading gold, precious stones, and spices (Ezekiel 27:22–24).

Though these peoples were then engaged in wars on many fronts, the queen entertained peaceful intentions. Thoroughly quizzed, King Solomon answered all her questions without difficulty. Much impressed, she in turn sang his praises, proclaiming that he was even wiser than people said. "Blessed by Yahweh your God who has showed you his favor by setting you on the throne of Israel! Because of Yahweh's everlasting love for Israel, he has made you king to administer law and justice" (1 Kings 10:9).

The queen of sheba

None of Israel's neighbors had ever spoken in this manner. They exchanged gifts and then the queen of Sheba returned whence she came.

Seldom miserly with details of this nature, the Bible fails to make clear if their relationship was amorous, and does not even make reference to the queen's beauty. The queen's neighbors on the other side of the Red Sea, the Ethiopians, recount the loves of the queen of Sheba and Solomon, even naming the outcome of their union: an ancestor of their emperors named Menelik.[3]

The queen of Sheba was, however, never to be forgotten in Israel. Approximately ten centuries later, when the Pharisees asked him to perform a miracle to prove his authority, Jesus answered that the queen had shown more faith than them: "On Judgement Day the Queen of the South will appear against this generation and be its condemnation, because she came from the ends of the earth to hear the wisdom of Solomon; and look, there is something greater than Solomon here" (Matthew 12:42).

A great conqueror and builder, Solomon left such a large realm that soon after his death his heirs fell to quarreling.

His son and designated successor, Roboam, was already reigning in Judah. However Judah "did what is displeasing to Yahweh, arousing his resentment more than his ancestors by all the sins they had committed" (1 Kings 14:22). In other words, Roboam worshipped alien gods and did nothing to stem the tide of sacred prostitution.

Soon, the North and the South again separated, the pretext being a tax Solomon had increased, which the tribes of the North wanted to see reduced.

Though a skillful politician, the seventh king of the North, Achab, would have left little mark in history had he not married a Phoenician—a pagan in the eyes of the Hebrews—called Jezabel. Jezabel's father was a follower of Baal, at once "lord of heaven" and "prince of the earth," who was reborn each year and whose cult was gaining ground at the time. He was a god held in opprobrium by the prophets, however.

Jezabel's father had appointed his daughter "high priestess of Baal," and she—clearly a woman of character—had not changed her beliefs on marrying Achab. On the contrary.

According to the prophet Elijah (1 Kings 18:19), she had even found room at court for some four hundred and fifty prophets of Baal and four hundred prophets of Asherah (a female deity considered "mother of the gods") and invited them to her table. Moreover, she had a number of prophets faithful to Yahweh put to death, though the master of the palace managed to save a further hundred. Clearly both camps boasted a posse of prophets.

Jezabel

As a believer in Yahweh, Elijah issued a challenge to Achab: let the pagan prophets protected by Queen Jezabel gather together before the people at Mount Carmel; let them built a bonfire and put a bull on top of it. He, Elijah, would do the same thing. Let them call upon Baal as he calls upon Yahweh. And let it be seen which God answers their prayers first.

The people found the proposal interesting, so the prophets found themselves cornered.

The curtain then rises on one of the most astonishing scenes in the entire Bible. The prophets of Baal dance all morning, "performing a hobbling dance" before their altar, beseeching their god, but nothing happens.

Elijah laughs at their expense: " 'Call louder,' he said, 'for he is a god: he is preoccupied or he is busy, or he has gone on a journey; perhaps he is asleep and needs to be woken up' " (1 Kings 18:27).

The author of this account (manifestly not very objective) then tells how they "shouted louder and gashed themselves, as their custom was," but to no avail.

Elijah then starts by saturating the fire and filling the surrounding trench with water. As he prays to Yahweh, fire comes down and devours everything, even the stones and the ground, and the water in the trench around the pyre. Not satisfied with ridiculing the losers, the prophet of Yahweh then has the people capture them and slash their throats. In the war between disciples of Yahweh and Baal, it appears that the defeated were often slain. In judging Jezabel's depravity and her intrigues, one obviously needs to keep such traditions in mind.

The author of the book of Kings, however, places great stress on the queen's misdeeds. For example, the book describes how she had a certain Naboth

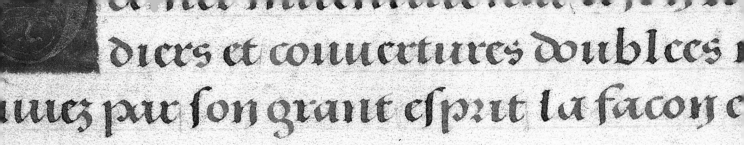

assassinated because he did not want to hand over a vineyard that he rightfully owned. Compared to the countless bloodbaths recounted in the Bible, this affair seems almost trifling, but Jezabel was assisted in her plot by two "scoundrels"— actually, "men of Belial" (that is, the devil). Her especial crime was, in fact, having introduced the pagan worship of Baal into the country and having placed it on an official footing (1 Kings 21:4–16).

Athaliah

Jehu, Achab's successor, took it upon himself to put an end to this situation. One day, passing before the palace, Jezabel, in full makeup and jewelry, leans out of the window and goads him. He has her thrown to the ground and then he "rode over her" (2 Kings 9:33).

When he comes to bury her—she was, after all, "daughter of a king"—only her hands, skull, and feet remain. These parts are thrown to the dogs.

Her daughter, Athaliah, fared scarcely any better. Ambitious, she married Joram, heir to the kingdom of the South, Judah. She exerted a pernicious influence over her husband, the Bible tells us (2 Chronicles 21:6), without further precision. After the death of Joram she went on to hoodwink his son, Ochozias, now king. He in turn was executed by Jehu, who, in Samaria, had "seventy sons" of Achab assassinated. Athaliah then seized the reins of the country, because none of the late king's descendants was "strong enough to rule" (2 Chronicles 22:9).

However, to make sure her power remained absolute, she slaughtered all "the royal stock of the house of Judah," down to her own grandchildren. The only survivor was the young Joas, still at the breast, who was hidden in the Temple by an aunt.

Everything opposed the reign of Athaliah: she was foreign and a pagan, like her mother—and a woman to boot. Nevertheless, she exercised all the powers of a king and became the only woman the Bible records as having "governed the country" (2 Chronicles 22:12).

Obviously, the priests could not countenance a female pagan ruling over Jerusalem for long. After a reign of six years, one of them, named Jehoiada, decided to call a halt to the situation. He gathered all the priests in the kingdom, as well as their flock, and handed out the weapons of David that were stored in the Temple.

Alerted, Athaliah, in a courageous act, marched off to the Temple. They did not slay her there, however, but at the gates to her palace, destroying the rival temple that she had erected to the glory of Baal (2 Chronicles 23:1–17).

Shortly afterwards, the young king Joas organized a collection to restore the Temple of Jerusalem, but the grandson of Athaliah (and great-grandson of Jezabel) also abandoned the worship of Yahweh in his turn. Perhaps this was because, as a note in the Bible of Jerusalem suggests, he wanted to shake off "priestly supervision and follow his lay advisers." He even killed Zachariah, son of Jehoiada, who had restored him to the throne with his own hand. As a punishment, Yahweh unleashed against him an Aramaean army that laid waste to the kingdom of Judah (2 Chronicles 24:17–25).

The inspiration behind many works of fiction, Jezabel and Athaliah left a stain on the history of the Israelites. Because they were women? One cannot deduce as much from the texts, as the authors prefer to place the stress on the women's paganism. After all, Yahweh's priority is to make sure his people remain true to him.

One other story of a queen has nourished the imagination: that of Esther.[4] But her tale is very different.

Esther was a Jewess living in the empire of Ahasuerus, which extended from India to Ethiopia, covering seven hundred and twenty-five provinces. A great beauty, she was born into a notable Jewish family, who were deported to Babylon by Nebuchadnezzar in the sixth century BCE.

esther

Ahasuerus, however, had recently repudiated his wife, Vashti, for disobedience. Summoning his officials and servants, he sends them out into his vast empire to find a worthy replacement.

Esther lines up among the candidates, without confessing her Hebrew origins, passes the preliminary examinations and undergoes a year of training in the harem in makeup and beautification, before being presented to the sovereign. Dazzled, the monarch at once places a diadem on her head before throwing a fabulous party to celebrate their wedding.

Esther has an uncle, Mordecai, an official, who advises her to conceal her Judaic background. All goes well until the day the king names as grand vizier a wildly proud man called Haman.

Mordecai makes the mistake of refusing to kneel as his colleagues have done when the vizier passes. Furious, Haman decides on the root-and-branch solution of eliminating all the Hebrews from the empire, a proposal accepted by Ahasuerus.

Mordecai tells his niece, the queen that she must intervene. But this idea is not very easy to put into practice as a law punishes by death any person—even a queen—who presents themselves before the King of Kings without a summons. Esther prepares to break this rule, praying, fasting, and dressing in all her finery.

"In full splendor of her beauty," she intrudes on the royal presence. Initially shocked and enraged, the king then takes her in his arms and promises her whatever she desires.

But her sole request is to be permitted to attend a "banquet" on the following day to which Haman has been invited. That night, Ahasuerus opportunely recalls that Mordecai one day saved his life: in the Bible, dreams are often highly informative.

As Ahasuerus, Haman, and Esther feast, Esther reveals her origins to the king and begs him to rescind the decree to exterminate the Jews. Ahasuerus loves her so much that he accedes to her request. The grand vizier, discovered by the king acting improperly before the queen, is hanged from the same gibbet he had erected for Mordecai. On the day set for their extermination, meanwhile, the Jews massacre all their adversaries.

This narrative, which experts see as having little historical veracity, is intended above all to demonstrate how Yahweh, who has pity for the persecuted in every age, raises up the weak and punishes the proud, saves His people and crushes their enemies.

victims and temptresses

*An opportunity came on Herod's birthday
when he gave a banquet for the nobles
of his court, for his army officers and for the
leading figures in Galilee. When the daughter
of this same Herodias came in and danced,
she delighted Herod and his guests; so the king
said to the girl, "Ask me anything you like and
I will give it you." … "I want you to give me
John the Baptist's head, immediately, on a dish."
The king was deeply distressed but, thinking
of the oaths he had sworn and of his guests,
he was reluctant to break his word to her.
At once the king sent one of the bodyguard with
orders to bring John's head. The man went off
and beheaded him in the prison; then he brought
the head on a dish and gave it to the girl, and
the girl gave it to her mother.*
(Mark 6:21–28)

Pages 104–05
After Frans Francken the Younger,
The Feast of Herod, seventeenth century,
Musée des Beaux-Arts, Dole

Guido Reni, *The Massacre
of the Innocents* (detail), c. 1611–12,
Pinacoteca Nazionale, Bologna

victims and temptresses

Eve | Jephthah's daughter | The judgment of Solomon | Job's wife |
Putiphar's wife | Delilah | Salome | The Massacre of the Innocents

The history of the "chosen" people—some authorities prefer the term "elect"—has included more than its fair share of dramatic situations. Several are associated with women—as victims, as heroines, or as malefactors.

The authors of the biblical books show themselves in general rather indulgent with respect to women, such as Sarah, Judith, or Hannah, even if some were of foreign origin, like Ruth. Their preference is certainly for Hebrew women, though, since it is their act of bringing children into the world that ensures the survival of their stock.

A strand of misogyny is evident, however, in a non-canonical text such as the book of Enoch, which is of unknown origin since Enoch, Noah's grandfather, is obviously not the author. That book tells how some angels were "deposed" because they found women so attractive that they wanted to descend onto earth to "fornicate" with them.

One of the most severe judgments on womankind was, of course, the one handed out to Eve, the first woman of all, who was responsible, according to the usual interpretation of Genesis, for the first "drama" in human history. And yet, in Christian eyes, it was again a woman, Mary, who, by giving birth to Jesus, plays a crucial role in the salvation of humanity.

Other women were involved in spectacular incidents. They come from all walks of life: the wife (whose name the Bible does not even mention) of the dignitary Job; the two anonymous prostitutes who appealed to Solomon to judge which of them was the mother of a child; Jephthah's daughter, killed by her own father, a "valiant warrior" who rose to become a general; then, in the New Testament, the mothers of the innocent babes of Bethlehem whom Herod murdered.

Excepting Eve and Mary, none is more famous than Delilah. Beautiful, as the women of the Bible frequently are in the eyes of its writers, her notoriety stems from her role in the long and complicated story of Samson, a man whose life was involved with three women who were—as so often—all foreigners.

In what was a far from homogenous region, relationships between the sexes had become a complex issue. Since its Covenant with God, the people of Abraham were obsessed by two imperatives: on the one hand, they had to survive and reproduce, so as to bear the Good News; on the other, they had to avoid relations with any who did not share their faith in the one true God.

Thus, when old Abraham sends his servant Eleazar to search far and wide for a wife for his son Isaac, it is because he needs a daughter-in-law from his own people. In her turn, Rebekah (Rebecca) is said to have felt "bitter disappointment" when her elder son, Esau, took a foreign wife. He was eventually to pay the price.

Foreign females, adorers of alien gods, are a priori suspect. And it was another foreign woman, the wife of Putiphar, who tried to distract the fourth patriarch, Joseph, son of Jacob, from his mission. Yet evil does not invariably originate with outsiders or women: after all, Jacob's own brothers had tried to eliminate him.

The encounter between Adam and Eve, as recounted in Genesis, is rather odd. Essentially, humanity had started out as a single entity. But God, who *is* love, knows that love is predicated on relationships between two people.

He thus extracts a rib from a human being who was up to that point man and woman in one, before he "closed the flesh up again," as the text of Genesis has it (Genesis 2:21). Yet, when God introduces woman to man (he had remained unconscious during the operation), Adam merely exclaims: "This one is at last bone of my bones and flesh of my flesh! She is to be called Woman, because she was taken from Man" (Genesis 2:23).

In the whole scene, man thinks only of himself: He does not thank God for giving him a partner, does not speak to woman; he is simply proud that she was "taken" from him, and, in what is a sign of power, names her.

Similarly, here and in the following verses—and this is an important clue, even if no hard-and-fast conclusions can be drawn—the first to address a word to woman is the serpent. But the serpent is not identical to the devil: no verse in Genesis compares the reptile to Satan. It is introduced only as "the most subtle of all the wild animals that Yahweh God had made" (Genesis 3:1).

A number of questions arise: since man was not the first to turn to Eve, perhaps the fault lies with him; or, if that term seems too strong, perhaps he disappointed God, who had intended for them to enter into a loving union. Furthermore, if a tree of good and evil exists, doesn't this mean that evil is already in wait, if not as a reality, at least as a virtuality, a possibility already actualized in that "most subtle of all the wild animals." Thirdly: why would God have placed the perfect opportunity for man and woman to disobey him "in the middle of the garden"? To test them? But that would hardly square with the image of God conveyed by the prophets and especially by Jesus who, moreover, never mentioned original sin.

Today a number of specialists are of the opinion that the account in Genesis signifies above all that evil has been present since man has been man (and perhaps even prior to that) and that the freedom the love of God grants to humankind presupposes a potential for evil-doing; for if not, man would be like a robot preprogrammed to sing the praises of his creator.

Yahweh, moreover, when He drives the couple out of the Garden of Eden, does not lambast Eve. He refers to "the intense pain in childbearing" and tells woman that man "will dominate" her (Genesis 3:16); though, if one can judge by his first words, Adam already had a penchant for despotism.

As we have remarked, Yahweh even protects the first murderer, Cain, by putting on him "a sign," announcing: "Whoever kills Cain will suffer a sevenfold vengeance" (Genesis 4:15).

Corresponding to a need for clarification, the whole story, it seems, is in keeping with the psychology and the traditions of a people from a very remote epoch. Being the mother of all humanity, Eve is the

Facing page
Paul Sérusier, *Breton Eve*
(or *Mélancolie*), c. 1891,
Musée d'Orsay, Paris

best-known woman in the Old Testament, and yet her inner thoughts remain undisclosed.

A similar quandary arises with respect to the daughter of Jephthah, if on a different level. With a name meaning "liberated God," Jephthah was a "judge" of Israel who probably lived in the eleventh century BCE.

The son of a prostitute, he had become a worthy "of the country of Gilead," i.e., Transjordan, then inhabited by Israelite tribes. After his birth, his father wed, and the sons born of this marriage drove out Jephthah, their brother, for the meanest of reasons: they did not want to share their progenitor's inheritance.

Jephthah thus had to seek his fortune elsewhere and moved nearer the Syrian plain, a place invested by lowlife and gangs of plunderers and mercenaries. There, he made a name for himself and became a famous "chieftain." In this respect, he was an incarnation of malevolence. At that juncture, the Ammonites and Moabites, those perennial enemies of Israel, invaded the land of Gilead, whose inhabitants, seized by terror, could only imagine one man capable of rallying the troops and saving them: Jephthah.

He accepts the challenge, but he is not one to offer such services for free. If he wins, he demands recognition as the leader of the country. And, as he is far from sure of his victory, he makes a vow: "If you deliver the Ammonites into my grasp, the first thing to come out of the doors of my house when I return … shall belong to Yahweh and I shall sacrifice it as a burnt offering" (Judges 11:30–31).

Jephthah's daughter

In other words, he announces that he will, with the assistance of Yahweh, dispatch at least one of his new subjects—a vow all too reminiscent of some ghastly trade-off, as the rest of story will bear out.

After he duly crushes the Ammonites, Jephthah—covered in glory—makes his way back to his house in high spirits. But who comes out to meet him first, dancing to the sound of the tambourine? His own daughter, his only child! She is aware of what she is doing, since Jephthah's vow was made publicly (some translations say he "opened his mouth wide towards the Lord"). If he is determined to exercise the absolute power he craves, Jephthah will be forced to hold to his awful promise.

Yet Jephthah, in spite of his ambition and his right of life and death, is also a loving father. Moreover, since she is his only child, if he slaughters his daughter he will have no descendants. His need for offspring—that obsession among the men of the Bible—will thus not be realized. The great headman gives vent to his misery.

But what was his daughter hoping to achieve? By arranging to be the first person her father saw, was she trying to flout his ambition or to show him the folly of his vow or to protect the other occupants of the household? In that case, she represents an incarnation of good; one aware of Jephthah's vice, who offers herself as a willing victim to save others. Or was she hoping that her father's love would override his thirst for power and that he would revoke his vow and abandon his mad ambition? She even asks him for a deadline of two months before being put

to death, which he grants her. But, by the end of that stay of execution, he has not changed his mind and she is killed. Jephthah clearly does not understand that Yahweh does not call for human sacrifice: so he is not just ambitious, he is obtuse.

King Solomon was very different. Son of and successor to David, like his father he reigned in Israel for exactly forty years—a sacred number. Yahweh, it is true, favors him. He appears to him in a dream at the onset of his reign, saying: "Ask what you would me to give you." Whereas, as the Bible often shows, many would have requested power and glory, Solomon evinces great humility: "I am a very young man," he answers, "unskilled in leadership.... So give your servant a heart to understand how to govern your people, to discern between good and evil" (1 Kings 3:7–9). And this Yahweh grants amply.

According to the author of the narrative, the Lord responded: "I give you a heart wise and shrewd as no one has had before and no one will have after you" (1 Kings 3:12). And, for good measure, God gives Solomon lots besides: "riches and glory," and—as long as he behaves—"a long life."

Immediately after this conversation, our author appends a scene apparently designed to exemplify Solomon's gifts. This is the story of two prostitutes who each swear they are the mother of the same child. They live, alone, in one and the same house, and give birth only three days apart. Unfortunately, one of the newborns dies because, as the first women alleges, the other woman rolled over on him during the night. The other child is alive and both claim him as her own. From the text, it appears there was a lot of screaming and shouting. Solomon sits in judgment: In a trice, he calls for a sword and orders one of his servants to slice the body of the baby into two and give each woman half. The real mother then howls in protest and reneges on her demand: "I beg you ... let them give her the child," she beseeches (1 Kings 3:26). Overwrought and unyielding, the other woman exclaims: "He shall belong to neither of us. Cut him in half!" The king of course understands at once that the first must be the true mother, and so hands her the baby.

The tale does not relate how the two women (who up to that point had lived together) reacted, and there is not one word of compassion for the mother, who, even though she subsequently lied, had lost an infant. The stress is placed entirely on how the populace sees Solomon as possessing "divine wisdom for dispensing justice" (1 Kings 3:28); the preeminent quality demanded of a king.

The Bible devotes a handful of lines to another woman who bends the knee before evil, tellingly not even mentioning her name. This is Job's wife, a figure most often omitted from commentaries on the eponymous book in which she appears.

The beginning of the story is well known. A wealthy dignitary, Job, had "shunned evil" and possessed vast herds that made him the "most prosperous of all the

The judgment of solomon

"Job tormented by the Devil,"
illumination from a book of hours
illustrating the story of Job, c. 1500,
private collection

"Job cursed by his wife,"
illumination from a book of hours
illustrating the story of Job, c. 1500,
private collection

Sons of the East" (Job 1:3). He was also a "sound and honest man who feared God."

In general, his rather bizarre family life is skirted over: Job has seven sons and three daughters, and, as the Bible states, "it was the custom of his sons to hold banquets in one another's house in turn and to invite their three sisters to eat and drink with them" (Job 1:4). As the father entertains suspicions of debauchery, after each feast he "would send for them to come and be purified, and … at dawn on the following day, would make a burnt offering for each." "Perhaps," he laments, "my sons have sinned [with their sisters?] and in their heart blasphemed."

The biblical text mentions no more of this, going on to tell how Satan, who "attend[ed] on Yahweh," suggested setting a trap for Job. His reasoning is simplicity itself: if such a rich landowner seems committed to Yahweh, it is only because he feels favored by the Lord. If, on the other hand, he was struck by misfortune, then he will curse Yahweh "to [His] face." So why not put him through an ordeal to measure the true depth of his faith?

Yahweh takes up Satan's challenge. The devil may strike Job's property with all the ills he can think of, but the patriarch himself must be spared. And Satan, that courtier of Yahweh's (a fact often conveniently forgotten), sets to work.

The catastrophes come thick and fast: first all his livestock is destroyed; then his sons and daughters are killed by a "gale" as they sit "eating and drinking in their eldest brother's house" (Job 1:13).

Job's wife

Ruined, Job bears all these misfortunes with dignity and faith. But Satan returns to the charge: "Lay a finger on his bones and his flesh: I warrant you that he will curse you to your face" (Job 2:5). Yahweh, who has total trust in Job, accepts this escalation, and Satan strikes the patriarch with "malignant ulcers"—leprosy perhaps.

It is at this point that Job's wife intervenes. As he leaves to go and sit among the ashes (that is, at the village garbage dump), she comes up and asks him to curse the Lord. Job answers: "That is how a fool of a woman talks…. If we must take happiness from God's hand, must we not take sorrow too?" (Job 2:10).

The woman vanishes from the story. Three "friends" of Job then file past, rehashing traditional answers to the question of evil: If Job is suffering now, it is because he has sinned, or it was perhaps his ancestors; moreover, suffering can teach us something. A fourth character, Elihu, comes in turn to reiterate their points in different language. Then, Yahweh intervenes, underlining the mysteries of Creation, recalling his mastery over the forces of evil and contradicting the analysis of the three "sages." Job, far from blaspheming against God as advised by his wife, bows down to Him. Subsequently, he recovers all his property and more besides, and has "seven daughters and three sons" (Job 42:12).

Yet Job's wife makes no reappearance. It has been clear from the start, however, that she was absent and unconcerned about her children's behavior. She is perhaps unfaithful to Yahweh, as she is ready to curse

Facing page
"Joseph fleeing Putiphar's wife,"
miniature from *De decem
praeceptis divinae legis* (detail), 1279,
private collection, Milan

Him, as well as to her husband; she is of no comfort to him when misfortune strikes. She is not the origin of his ills, but she is eager to join the ranks of the wrongdoers if they look like winning.

Other biblical women are more active in their malevolence, for instance, the wife of Putiphar, who was a eunuch in the service of Pharaoh at the time when Jacob's eleventh son, Joseph, was sold to Pharaoh by his brothers. Joseph is wise, a saint, a bearer of the divine word. Soon noticed by the entourage around Pharaoh, he becomes his chief adviser, later becoming instrumental in assuring the release of his Jewish brothers from slavery.

putiphar's wife

In addition, Joseph is "well-built and handsome" (Genesis 39:6). Putiphar's wife (whose name the authors of the narrative do not bother to provide) is soon besotted, and literally orders him to come to her bed (Genesis 39:7). Joseph resists; if he were to accept, he might become the master in a powerful house, but he would certainly remain the mistress's slave. He has to repel the lady's advances repeatedly, but she won't take "no" for an answer. One day, when they are alone in the palace, she suddenly tries to embrace him. As Joseph flees, she grabs his garment and is left holding it. She then uses this as evidence that the young man tried to have his way with *her*. The trick hoodwinks everyone and Joseph is punished, thrown into jail with other prisoners of the king. He soon impresses the head jailer, though, and begins enjoying preferential treatment. In the end he rises to become "chancellor" at Pharaoh's palace.

This passage from Genesis might well have been quickly forgotten had it not provided ample scope for artists to show a nude woman—the soon infamous wife of Putiphar—at times when such representations were practically forbidden, save in a mythological or biblical context.

The story of Delilah is also often depicted, and for similar reasons. Her lover Samson was a popular hero, an invincible champion whose remarkable exploits were legendary, but also (as misogynist commentators allege) a victim "of feminine wiles" on no fewer than three occasions.

His mother had been infertile, just like Sarah, Rachel, and so many others. And, like them, this woman—whose name is again not mentioned in the Bible—is told of the imminent birth of a son by an angel: Yahweh, in point of fact.

This prospect is only half welcome, because she learns that this son is to become a Nazirite (from *nazir*, "separate"), and personally dedicated to Yahweh. This status brought with it various obligations: to avoid wine and any product of the vine; not to let the hair grow long as a visible sign of consecration;

delilah

never to approach a corpse, as this fosters "impurity" which has to be cleansed by a slew of ritual sacrifices. The angel who announces the birth of Samson moreover informs the mother-to-be that her son is *nazir* even in the womb—which means that the rules apply to her too.

Guercino, *Samson and Delilah*,
c. 1657, Musée des Beaux-Arts,
Strasbourg

Facing page
Gustave Moreau, *Delilah
with the Ibis* (detail), 1880,
Musée Gustave-Moreau, Paris

She complies and soon her son, inspired by the spirit of the Lord from an early age, becomes a fearsome warrior, inflicting countless defeats and humiliations on the Philistines, who were fighting over territory with the Hebrews. But Samson takes it into his head to marry another of those foreign girls.

The wedding comes to nothing, though, because on the appointed day the father substitutes another girl for his daughter. Filled with the desire for vengeance, Samson embarks on a veritable massacre of the Philistines, causing "great havoc" (Judges 15:8) among them.

Immensely strong and far from stupid, Samson's fondness for women nonetheless one day induces him to lower his guard with a prostitute from Gaza, a city which, despite repeated Israelite attacks, was still in Philistine hands. The news of Samson's arrival quickly spread, and while he was carousing with the prostitute, the inhabitants encircle the house. But remaining alert and on his guard, Samson sneaks out in the middle of the night and surprises his adversaries; his strength is such that, not content with simply putting them to flight, he rips off the gates to the city and carries them off to a hill dozens of miles away.

But a third woman does get the better of him: Delilah, of course. For once the Bible provides her with a name, perhaps because various legends had been absorbed into the story even before it took its place in the book of Judges.

Once Samson is in Delilah's clutches, the Philistine princes come to the young woman and promise her a huge reward if she manages to wangle out of him the secret of his superhuman strength.

Samson is wary and prevaricates, but she badgers him so much and for so long that he ends up revealing that his power resides in his hair, since he is *nazir* to the Lord. He then falls asleep on Delilah's lap and she shaves his head.

The Philistines seize him, put out his eyes, and drag him to Gaza, where he is condemned to turn a grinding stone in the prison. Now the superhuman is an object of derision. But the Philistines forgot that hair grows back, and one feast day they conduct him into the temple of their god, Dagon, whose memory is still recalled in the occasional place name in Palestine. Intent on poking fun at him, they get him to perform tricks. But the young boy who was "leading him by the hand" has the bright idea of standing Samson between two columns similar to those he has been in the habit of toppling. Samson asks for permission to touch them. His request granted, Samson, leaning against the pillars, calls upon Yahweh: "Let me die with the Philistines!" (Judges 16:30). The mob perishes, crushed beneath the temple as Samson brings it down, slaughtering more enemies than "he had done to death during his life."

Our author does not tell us whether Delilah was among the victims, as he focuses rather on showing that, if Israel, like Samson, can fail in its duty, Yahweh remains faithful to his straying *nazir*.

The New Testament tells the tale of a girl whose name is not recorded in the Gospel texts of Matthew

and Mark, just as the Old Testament fails to provide that of Putiphar's wife. Her name is only known from the first-century Jewish historian, Flavius Josephus: this is Salome, who has inspired painters even more than the wife of Putiphar. In the first century of the Christian era, King Herod, the great and fierce Herod, died, and his heirs were left to split his inheritance.

One of them, likewise named Herod, lives with Herodias, the wife of his brother, Philip. This was an unacceptable situation morally and legally, and John the Baptist reproaches the king publicly. Herodias, who detests him, thinks this a perfect pretext for having the prophet executed.

But the sovereign cannot bring himself to do it. Perhaps because he is worried about the reaction of the people or, if the evangelist St. Mark is to be believed (Mark 6:20), because he "liked to listen" to the Baptist preaching.

However, as Mark also writes, the "opportunity came" at a great banquet thrown to celebrate Herod's birthday. A pretty dancer appears: Herodias' daughter. The monarch is so bedazzled that he promises to give her whatever she desires. Overcome, the girl asks for advice from her mother, who has the answer ready: what she wants is the head of John the Baptist. The dancer returns to Herod to announce her choice.

The king, "deeply distressed" (Mark 6:26), but unable to go back on his word before the assembled crowd, orders a guard to bring him John's head on a platter, and the Baptist is decapitated.

Herod's act was indeed brutal, but he fulfilled his promise with a heavy heart.

salome

Strangely Flavius Josephus, who hated Herod and his brood, makes no mention of another drama that must have struck many women in the same period: the Massacre of the Innocents.

Only the evangelist Saint Matthew (Matthew 2:1–12) recounts the events. The protagonists—the Magi, the wise men sometimes described as kings or even astrologers—having seen a sign in the sky, arrive from the Orient to worship Jesus. They are then foolhardy enough to visit Herod, a man who is easily offended and obsessed by plots, to ask him where the king of the Jews might be born.

Herod, who in this account appears as a complete ignoramus, consults some holy men, who refer to a prophecy in Micah (from the eighth century BCE), which declares rather curtly: "But you, Bethlehem-Ephrathah, the least of the clans of Judah, from you will come to me a future ruler of Israel" (Micah 5:1). Ephrathah, initially the name of one of the many Jewish clans, also means "the fertile." To Herod, the danger is clear: he dispatches his visitors on a mission: they are to go and reconnoiter Bethlehem and report back to him.

They set off, find Jesus and Mary, and offer their gold and their perfumes of Arabia. But, informed in a dream of Herod's evil intent, they take care not to pass back via Jerusalem.

Herod, furious at being fooled by the wise men, orders all the male children in Bethlehem and its surrounding district, aged two years old or under, to be killed, reckoning by the date he had been careful to ask the wise men (Matthew 2:16).

The story is a horrendous one: the pain of the mothers as their babies are torn from their breasts by soldiers and put to the sword can only be imagined.

Later, in the fifth century, the Fathers of the Church, Origen and Saint Leo the Great, added the detail that

The Massacre of the Innocents

there were three Magi. By the seventh century, they had acquired the names of Melchior, Balthazar, and Gaspar; while by the fifteenth, they each had a different skin color: Melchior was white, Balthazar black, and Gaspar yellow, between them symbolizing the whole world.

Historians have long questioned the veracity of this story (nowhere else is any trace of so a great massacre found), but the Church holds it to be true, seeing it as a sign that Jesus came for all humanity.

Creators of mosaics, column capitals, miniatures, and—from the fourteenth century on—paintings, have dedicated countless works to this Gospel passage, and among the greatest are those that focus on the mothers' suffering.

And if human pain is something even the doubter can comprehend, it is also understandable that many preachers compare the mothers' grief to the suffering Mary had to endure when her child was crucified.

women in jesus' entourage

There were some women watching from a distance. Among them were Mary of Magdala, Mary who was the mother of James the younger and Joset, and Salome. These used to follow him and look after him when he was in Galilee. And many other women were there who had come up to Jerusalem with him.
(Mark 15:40–41)

women in Jesus' entourage

The Samaritan | Joanna | The woman with the perfume |
The adulteress | Mary Magdalene | The Syro-Phoenician |
Jairus's daughter | The hemorrhaging woman | Martha and Mary | Mary

"Now it happened that after this he made his way through towns and villages preaching and proclaiming the good news of the kingdom of God. With him went the Twelve, as well as certain women who had been cured of evil spirits and ailments: Mary surnamed the Magdalene, from whom seven demons had gone out, Joanna the wife of Herod's steward Chuza, Susanna, and many others who provided for them out of their own resources."

These are the words with which the evangelist Luke (Luke 8:1–3) describes the women in Jesus' circle and the contingent of female helpers who accompanied the Apostles and provided financial assistance to the little group.

Gospel specialists underline the special interest Luke has in the role of the women in the group around Jesus, who, in the dark days of the trial and crucifixion, showed unflinching loyalty, in the main.

The links between women and Jesus have been obscured in some eyes by texts of Saint Paul such as Corinthians (1 Corinthians 11:3): "But I should like you to understand that the head of every man is Christ, the head of woman is man, and the head of Christ is God." Woman is thus placed on a lower rung of the ladder, being forbidden, for example, to pray bare-headed. Aspects of this attitude to women betray Paul's origins as a Pharisee. When Paul writes, "It is better to be married than to be burnt up" (1 Corinthians 7:9), for instance, it is clear that he considers marriage, the union between man and woman, as the lesser of two evils.

Jesus' position was very different and on occasion it led him to take issue precisely with the Pharisees;

as in the case of a woman with a disease that had left her "bent double and unable to stand" for twenty years.

One Sabbath, this unfortunate comes into the synagogue and Jesus calls her forward. Filled with compassion, he cures her, and the woman stands up straight. But the "president" of the synagogue reproaches him: there are six other days in the week, he says; it is not lawful to cure ills on the Sabbath. Jesus retorts: "Hypocrites! Is there one of you who does not untie his ox or his donkey from the manger on the Sabbath and take it out for watering?" At this, Luke continues, "all his adversaries were filled with confusion" (Luke 13:10–17).

Much the same can be said of the episode of the adulteress.

Similarly, when Jesus visits Martha and Mary after the death of their brother Lazarus, it was again to one of them, Martha, that he utters one of his most explicit affirmations of power. "I am the resurrection," he says. "Anyone who believes in me, even though that person dies, will live; and whoever lives and believes in me will never die. Do you believe this?" And she replies: "Yes, Lord; I believe that you are the Christ, the Son of God, the one who was to come into this world" (John 11:25–27). And, preceding the resurrection of Lazarus, it is this assertion that decided the adversaries of Jesus, the high priests and the Pharisees, to have him done away with.

And even after the Crucifixion, it is once more a woman, Mary Magdalene, he chooses to proclaim the Resurrection.

Odilon Redon,
Christ and the Samaritan Woman, c. 1895,
Städelsches Kunstinstitut, Frankfurt

Facing page
Byzantine icon, *Jesus and the Samaritan Woman at the Well* (detail),
late sixteenth century,
Paul Canellopoulos Collection, Athens

Jesus' benevolence with respect to women, it would seem, led some to extrapolate his views and his mission beyond what he would have wished. This is true in the case of an unnamed Samaritan woman.

She belongs to a people for whom the Hebrews had little time, considering them as pagans, as "possessed by the demon" even, despising them even more than the Philistines.

The Samaritans even have their own temple—an unacceptable state of affairs for their neighbors. Jesus explains to the woman that the fuss over the temple is a side issue, that one should not just adore God in one specific place since He is spirit and that it is thus in spirit that one must pray to Him. And he ends by explaining something he has not yet even told his disciples and companions. To one of her questions he replies that he is indeed the Messiah: "'That is who I am, I who speak to you'" (John 4:26).

One of the women who accompanied Jesus and his followers is, according to Luke, practically unknown and almost always passed over, yet she was one of the most fearless.

Joanna is the wife of Chuza, the steward of Herod Antipas, one of the seven sons of Herod the Great, the kinglet of Galilee. Though an aristocrat, Joanna shows no hesitation in leaving her up-to-date Greco-Roman-style house with its view over the lake to listen to and then to follow Jesus. When Luke refers to the group of women offering "their resources" to Jesus and his Apostles, Joanna must surely have been among the most important of these female donors. For someone in her position, however, such acts were not without risk, for both her and her husband, who was a kind of finance minister. She must have been a brave woman.

Unlike Jesus, the evangelists did not always look kindly on women, and they omit to mention her—save for the most "feminist," Luke. He also mentions how the women who came with Jesus "from Galilee" remained alone in Golgotha after his death when his body corpse was taken for burial by Joseph of Arimathaea. He goes on to list Joanna, together with Mary Magdalene, among the group which, on the third day at daybreak, went to the tomb "with spices and ointments."

The two then meet "two men in brilliant clothes," who announce the Resurrection to them. They run to repeat what they have seen to the Apostles, "but this story of theirs seemed like nonsense and they did not believe them" (Luke 24:11). If Joanna then vanishes from the New Testament of the Christians, her courage, faith, and constancy were far from negligible.

The samaritan

Joanna

Fra Angelico, *Deposition*,
Pala di Santa Trinità, c. 1437–40,
Museo di San Marco, Florence

Facing page
Emil Nolde, *The Women at the Tomb*
(detail), 1912, A. & E. Nolde Stiftung
Seebuell, Neukirchen

The most significant woman in Jesus' entourage at that time of his life was, however, Mary of Magdala. Magdala is the name of a large village near Capernaum on the shores of the Sea of Galilee. Some researchers have taken it upon themselves to allege that the inhabitants of this village were riddled with vice and so have regarded Mary Magdalene as a "sinner."

This defect is compounded by the fact that she is often—if unjustly—confused with the woman who, according again to Luke (7:36–50), burst into the house of a Pharisee where Jesus was dining. Falling down before him, she wept floods of tears, wiping his feet with her beautiful long tresses and anointing them with perfume. Nothing in the account, however, proves that this woman was indeed Mary Magdalene.

Investigators, moreover, have cast doubts on the likelihood of the whole scene. A woman known throughout the city for having "a bad name" could never have entered a Pharisee's house during a great feast without being stopped. All the more so since this particular Pharisee, forenamed Simon, was not much of a host, and that loose hair was indicative of impropriety in Jewish society at the time.

If the scene did actually take place, however, it makes plain a number of factors. Firstly, the Pharisee has so little interest in the woman that he doesn't even have her thrown out by his servants. He is concerned only with Jesus, with discovering something to accuse Him of. If Jesus is a prophet, Simon the Pharisee declares, he must surely know that the woman touching him is impure. And the woman knows she is sullied and is sorely unaware of her shame in a society obsessed with purity. This is why she does not dare to pour the perfume over Jesus' head: this would be, she thinks, too noble a gesture for a person such as her. At most she can humbly perfume his feet, as servants do for their masters, and as Jesus will do for his disciples on the occasion of the Last Supper.

But, on the evening in question, what does Jesus do? He begins by telling Simon the Pharisee a parable; it is the story of a man who has two debtors, one owing him ten times more than the other. As both were penniless, he waived both their debts. Jesus then asks Simon who of the two, in his opinion, would be the most grateful? The answer is obvious: the one who owed the greater sum.

Then he asks the Pharisee to look at the woman, not to avert his eyes—he who is pure—from the impure. And he asks him to compare her attitude with his own, who thinks he is right with God, since he follows all the commandments of the Law but never goes an inch further, being incapable of love and gratitude—which are qualities the woman, the "sinner" clearly has in abundance.

This same calling into question of the rigid observation of rules—of the Law—again emerges in an episode featuring another sinner, the woman taken in adultery.

The woman with the perfume

QUI SINE PECCATO EST VESTRUM, PRIMUS
IN ILLAM LAPIDEM MITTAT

Jesus is in Jerusalem, preaching in the Temple. One day, a woman is brought to him who has been caught *in flagrante*. The Law of Moses is unambiguous: such women must be stoned to death. Though at this period this punishment for adultery was falling into disuse, her captors could easily have taken her for stoning without referring to Jesus. They seem in fact chiefly concerned with setting a test for him, perhaps trying to make him do or say something unlawful.

Should the woman then be stoned? Jesus does not answer the question. Instead, he squats and writes something with his finger on the ground. They are not put off so easily and ask him again. Jesus stands up and declares: "Let the one among you who is guiltless be the first to throw a stone at her" (John 8:7).

Jesus bends down again and carries on writing. The men gradually withdraw one after the other—the oldest first, as John underlines with a smile.

But what did Jesus write? This is a question of heated debate. One hypothesis is intriguing. It recalls how Yahweh, too, had written the text of the Law with His finger, but on stone. Writing on sand then would seem to imply that the Law should be applied flexibly, adapted to the circumstances. In doing this, Jesus refers his questioners not to the letter of the Law, but to their consciences.

In inviting those who are without sin to declare themselves, Christ shifts from the legal to the moral arena. They understand the implication very well,

and, as they trudge off one by one, they betray their sinfulness.

Jesus does not condemn them, any more than he condemns the woman. For the Psalm (103:10) says: "[The Lord] does not treat us as our sins deserve, does not repay us as befits our offences." But Jesus does entreat the woman to sin no more.

The two stories—that of the sinner with the perfume and of the adulteress—therefore teach one and the same lesson: punctiliously observing the Law is not sufficient without true faith and love.

The adulteress

To return to Mary Magdalene; contrary to what is often alleged, she is definitely not the woman with the "bad name" who anointed Jesus. All four Gospels speak of her being present—like Joanna—at the time of Jesus' death, and of her visiting the tomb on Easter morning.

Luke alone reports that "seven demons" came out of her, without specifying where or how; neither does he mention when or how she met Christ. The most that can be said is that, for a number of scholars, it seems clear the act of exorcism was in fact the "curing" of an epileptic fit, but really all suppositions about Mary Magdalene's life are baseless.

On the other hand, she certainly plays a major role at the time of the Passion and Resurrection of Jesus. On the evening of his death, the crowd, after taking their fill of the spectacle of his suffering, is dispersed by the Roman legionaries. The master's disciples pretend not to know him and they slink off with the people, giving the high priests' henchmen a wide berth.

Johannes Pauwelszoon Moreelse,
The Repentant Mary Magdalene, (detail), 1630,
Musée des Beaux-Arts, Caen

Facing page
Cretan School, *Noli me tangere*
(detail), first half of the sixteenth century,
Museo dell'Istituto Ellenico, Venice

Practically, it's just the women who are left. They stand bolt upright, frozen into a block of pain, as if they find it impossible to desert Jesus, as if they are waiting for him to raise his voice and speak. Their hopes are dashed, but they still cannot watch him die like this, in the hours before Passover, before the feast day. Majestic in their dignity, they weep and pray to the Eternal.

Suddenly a man of noble bearing appears, accompanied by a Roman officer and surrounded by soldiers, who cuts down the body of the crucified from the Cross. He is wrapped in a shroud and borne off. Some of the women follow them, Mary Magdalene at their head. Finally, when the tomb is closed up, they withdraw, heartbroken.

Two days later (so after Passover), at dawn, Mary Magdalene runs to the tomb. This time, it is John who provides the most detailed account. She notices, he writes, that the stone has been rolled away and that the body of Jesus is no longer to be found in the tomb. She hurries off to inform Peter. He takes her word for it and, seeing how upset she is, follows her to the place. He too has to accept that Jesus' body has disappeared, but he is far from thinking of a resurrection and heads back.

Mary Magdalene, remains, however, near to the tomb, in tears. She suddenly catches sight of "two angels in white" (John 20:12) who ask her why she is weeping. "They have taken my Lord away," she replies.

Mary Magdalene

With these words, she turns away and sees a man standing there, but does not recognize him as Jesus.

Jesus says to her: "Woman, why are you weeping? Who are you looking for?" Mistaking him for the gardener, she answers: "Sir, if you have taken him away, tell me where you have put him, and I will go and remove him." But Jesus replies simply: "Mary!" and she recognizes him, exclaiming in Hebrew: "Rabbuni!" (John 20:14–16).

Saint John the Evangelist, who recounts this scene and uses the word "Rabbuni," is careful to gloss: "which means 'master'"—as if he was keen to exclude another interpretation. Everywhere else in the Gospels, however, the word for "master" is "rabbi." As a diminutive, *rabbuni* introduces a hint of familiarity or of tenderness.

Then Jesus asks Mary Magdalene to go and warn his disciples, who, according to the same evangelist, procrastinate. They have grown accustomed to going out rarely and to staying in at night "for fear of the Jews" (John here calls the enemies of Jesus the "Jews").

Actually, they don't really believe Mary Magdalene. Some of them were probably jealous that she was the first to have seen Christ resurrected. A text dating from the mid-second century, called *The Gospel of Mary*, claims that Peter then asks her: "Tell us the words that he [Jesus] said to you that you remember and which we do not know." If this text is to be believed, Peter thus acknowledges that a special intimacy existed between Mary and Jesus.

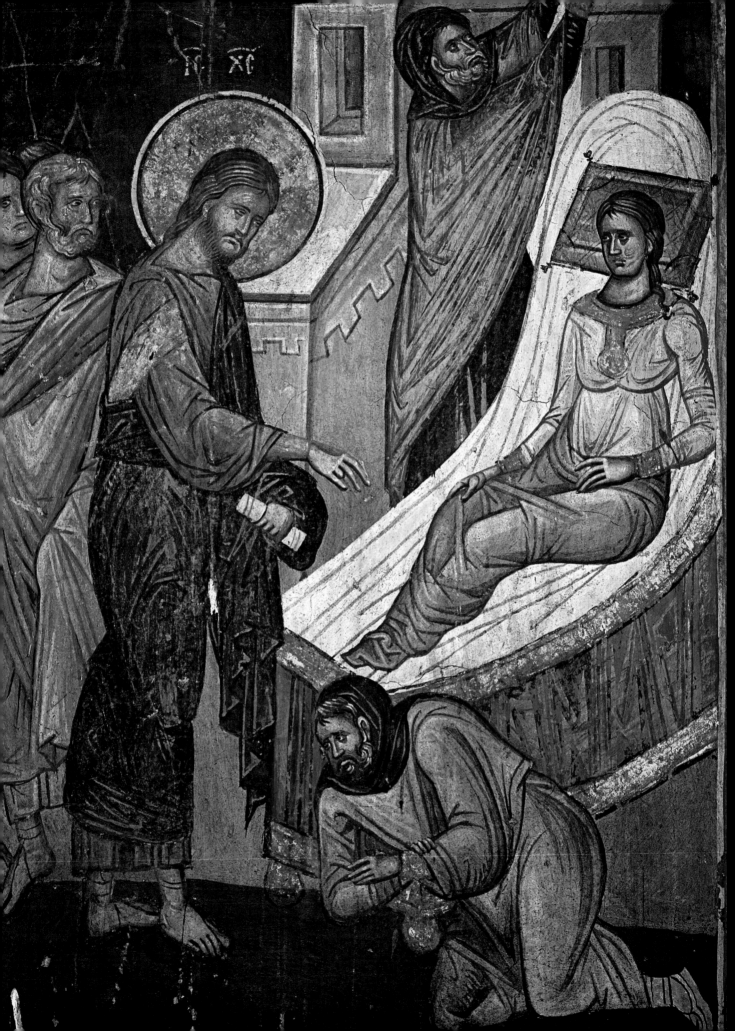

The language of her answer is somewhat involved, and Peter and his brother Andrew appear skeptical: "Is it possible that the Teacher [Jesus] discussed things with a woman of which we, we are unaware?"

The precise wording of the text can certainly be doubted, but it casts light on the difficulty men of the period—even those closest to him—felt in accepting the role Jesus gave to women.

It is true that the faith of these women in Jesus often appears more forcefully than among their male counterparts. The Gospels of Matthew and Mark even mention a woman who proclaims her faith in Jesus so loudly that the disciples find fault with it.

The woman concerned is a Syro-Phoenician (Mark 7:26), living in what is, in Jewish eyes, heathen territory. The evangelist Matthew, a Jew writing for a Jewish readership, calls her a "Canaanite," referring to the land of Canaan whose inhabitants were often at loggerheads with the people of Moses. By the first century, the adjective "Canaanite" was beginning to seem old-fashioned. If Matthew uses it, it is probably because he found the story a touch shocking.

Jesus seems to have started off rather uncompromisingly, at first (Matthew 15:22–28). Shouting and screaming, the Canaanite woman dogs Jesus' steps. Her daughter, she cries, "is tormented by a devil." Jesus does not even take the trouble to answer. She continues shouting, however, increasingly loudly in all probability, until the disciples ask him to get rid of this woman whose howling is getting on their nerves. So it is not for her benefit that they ask him to intervene, but for theirs.

He addresses her finally in these terms: "I was sent only to the lost sheep of the House of Israel." In other words, the salvation he brings is confined to the Jews alone. This surprising answer, considering the tenor of some of his other pronouncements—even in the Gospel of Saint Matthew—has given rise to a number of misleading commentaries on the text.

The episode continues. The woman now overtakes the group and in a rare show of the most profound faith, throws herself on the ground before Jesus. This time he answers her supplication with the words: "It is not fair to take the children's food and throw it to the little dogs." This is astonishingly severe: the "children" are, of course, the Jews, while the pagans are dubbed "dogs." The expression "little dogs" might be affectionate, but it surely must designate beings inferior to "children." In the Gospel of Mark (written before that of Matthew), Jesus says: "The children should be fed first" (Mark 7:27). Though it goes on to mention "little dogs," the expression "should be fed first" means that the Hebrews enjoy priority over salvation—but not exclusivity.

And this is what the woman understands. The puppies, she answers, eat the scraps that fall from the masters' table. In other words, there is food enough

The syro-phoenician

for them, too. Scraps, perhaps, but food nonetheless. Moreover, in speaking of "children," the Greek word employed is not *tekna*, meaning "children of one's descent," i.e., the Jews alone, but *pedia*, which applies to all children.

Jesus then answers with solemnity: "Woman, you have great faith! Let your desire be granted." And her daughter is at once cured.

How then can Jesus' initial reserve and even severity be explained? It is a lesson—indeed a double lesson—for all those who listen to, or now read, the Gospel of Matthew. On the one hand, the point is to show the faith of a woman from what is, according to the Hebrews, a godless country.

On the other, proceeding in stages, the text stresses how the word of Jesus, if at the outset addressed to the Jewish people, is actually universal; it also concerns the "little dogs," precisely those regarded by the Jews as heathens. And that their faith, too, can be "great."

Another woman who showed no less faith has already been mentioned. She was less vocal, simply hoping against hope. She had been suffering from a hemorrhage for twelve years, as if her periods never stopped.

In those days, according to the Law, women with a "discharge … of blood" were *niddah*: in other words, impure. They embodied, as Leviticus puts it, "uncleanness," and represented a danger to all they touched, men and children, fruit and unleavened

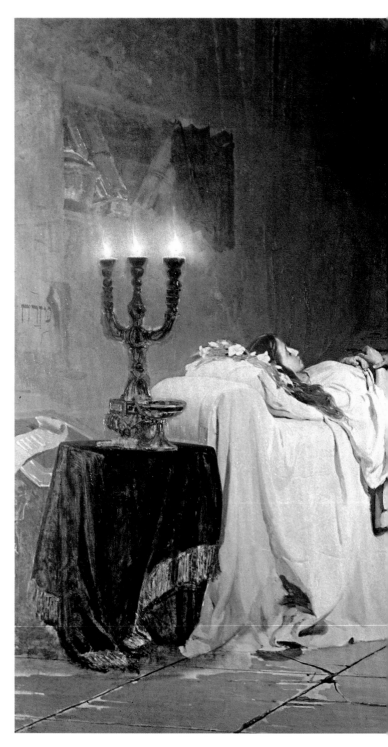

Jairus's daughter

bread, seats, and bedding (Leviticus 15:19–27). Soiled, they spread contamination.

For years then, this woman has been a pariah to her kith and kin. She has to tell her neighbors not to touch her and has to shout to children, who can't possibly understand, to keep out of her way. She would, however, so love to be like other people, to share in their lives, in their joys—in their misfortunes, even. She has seen countless itinerant magicians who ply their trade in the villages, and has even handed over money in the hope of a cure. But all in vain. She is sick at heart.

Then she hears people speak about the man from Nazareth, about Jesus, who is passing through the region. She hurries to the place, but Christ is busy with a certain Jairus, a president of the synagogue, who is in despair: his little daughter is at death's door. He begs Jesus: "Come and lay your hands upon her that she may be saved and may live," and Jesus accepts (Mark 5:23), rushing off in great haste to cure the girl. How did the hemorrhaging woman get to him through the hustle of the crowd? Pleading to be let through, she stretches out her hand to Jesus, propelled by an insane desire to touch him—no, not even his flesh, but just the edge of his cloak. But this folly, this confidence, this boundless hope will be enough.

For Jesus senses her hand. He turns, looking for someone who has barely brushed against his clothes. She stands trembling with joy and throws herself to his feet and blurts out her story. Jesus answers that it is her trust, her hope, her faith that has saved her, not him. And the woman is duly cured. This unnamed, hemorrhaging woman, can, because she has believed, now truly exist.

Martha and Mary

A family close to Jesus, headed by Lazarus, lived a few kilometers from Jerusalem in a village perched on the eastern slopes of the Mount of Olives. Now Lazarus had two sisters, Martha and Mary. If one may judge from the Gospel of Saint John, Jesus would sometimes pass the house (John 12:1–2), and, one day, a meal is offered in his honor. In describing this meal, Luke stresses that it was Martha who "welcomed him in" (Luke 10:38–42) before becoming "distracted with all the serving." Mary, meanwhile, was sitting at Christ's feet, asking him questions and drinking in his every word.

The Greek verb translated by "distracted" has a pejorative flavor, as if Martha were making too much fuss and crashing about preparing the meal. She, too, would like to listen, but, as a good housewife, she has to do what she can to make their guest comfortable.

She can't bear it anymore and turns on Jesus, telling him to put her sister straight. "Lord, do you not care that my sister is leaving me to do the serving all by myself? Please tell her to help me." Ordinarily, in the Gospel narratives, the disciples themselves do not talk to Jesus in this tone.

He does not upbraid her, though, instead pouring oil on troubled waters: "Martha … you worry and you fret about so many things, and yet so few are needed.… It is Mary who has chosen the better part."

This pronouncement is often interpreted as making a split between the active (Martha) and the contemplative life (Mary), a conclusion that has encouraged certain monks, for instance, to forsake action. Nonetheless, most commentators on the story rightly stress how both are equally necessary. It is clear, however, that for Luke, even though Martha is moved by the desire to honor Jesus by serving him well, it is Jesus' word that is the essential thing.

Of course another Mary served Jesus well, and that for thirty years. She too listened to him and conversed with him: his mother, the most famous woman in the New Testament. In point of fact, though, the text of the Bible hardly mentions her. The canonical Gospels say not a word about her parentage, her birth—nor even about how she met her husband Joseph.

Its authors record the origins of all the women they consider significant, with just two exceptions: Sarah, the wife of Abraham, and the Virgin. The Gospels and other texts making up the New Testament give scant information on the young woman's life. Matthew, who (with the feminist Luke) speaks about her at greatest length, devotes only 17 verses to her out of a total of the 1,068 comprising his Gospel.

John attaches prime importance to her, though—first of all due to the miracle at Cana, where, as the wine is running low, she urges her son to reveal himself, but is rebuffed by the famous: "My hour has not yet come." But most especially at the time of the crucifixion, where Saint John is the only one to signal her silent presence.

Yet Saint John, who has a fondness for symbols, stresses the fact that Jesus entrusts her to the "disciple whom he loved" (John 19:26), telling him: "This is your mother" (John 19:27).

It is no coincidence that the disciple in question is not named: in the Gospels, he never is, and there have been erudite discussions as to his identity. Perhaps he remains anonymous so as to represent the whole of humanity? So, with his last plea, Jesus designates Mary as the mother of all men.

Three centuries later, this young woman (less often quoted by name in the Gospels than Mary Magdalene) was proclaimed Mother of God (*theotokos*), and then Queen and Mother of the Church.

There is one aspect of her existence that is all too often forgotten, though: the simple fact that she lived thirty years with Jesus. The evangelists skip over it; except to recount (in Matthew and Luke) the birth of the Child and (in Luke alone) the twelve-year-old Jesus' discussions with the doctors at the Temple of Jerusalem, while his parents seek him high and low.

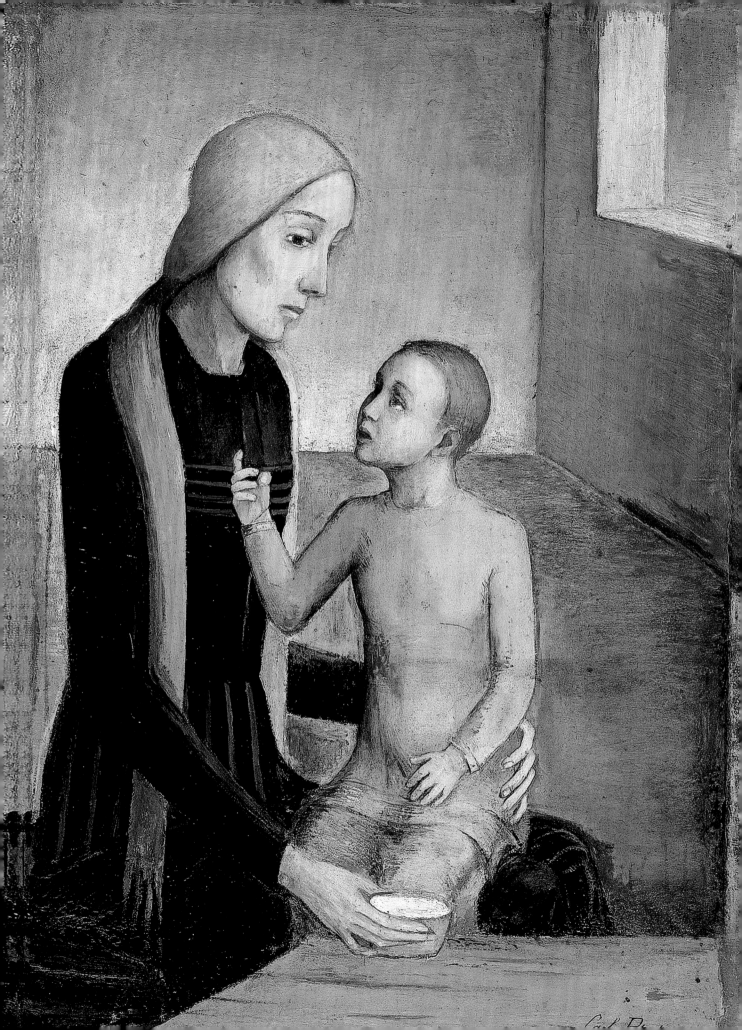

These three decades, however, reward further examination.

First, where are we? In Nazareth, a hamlet, where squalid houses are crammed together, leaving only narrow lanes through which packs of children of all ages scamper; where women congregate to do the washing and share the news, or trudge off into the fields to work; and also where Joseph takes Jesus to the synagogue, a place not only of worship but also of meeting and discussion.

If one believes in the Incarnation, if one accepts the divinity of Jesus, then he has to be imagined living in this place for thirty years. Yahweh in this world. God in Nazareth.

This boy was to transform the history of the world, and a woman called Mary (like so many others before and after her), brought him up day after day, with words, smiles, the occasional reprimand, with all she could teach, all she did in their daily life.

This mother is puzzled, of course, as her son is, but more than he is. And faced by assertions and attitudes that must have astonished her, she begs him to explain. And she will suffer by his words too.

One day, for example, he is out preaching in Capernaum and she needs to see him, to speak to him. He is informed, but answers: "Who are my mother and my brothers?" And, gazing out among those sitting around him, adds: "Here are my mother and my brothers. Anyone who does the will of God, that person is my brother and sister and mother" (Mark 3:31–35; Matthew 12:46–50; Luke 8:19–21). From now on, he will be entirely preoccupied by his mission.

Such is Mary. A woman who is worn down by the daily grind, whose hands are rough, whose eyes strain through the gloom of her hovel, her back bent by too many heavy burdens. In her heart, however, she nurtures a hope; she is known only through Jesus, because children act rather like mirrors.

If the mother of this young boy, who will prove to be the Son of God, was surely an exceptional, a luminous figure, she remains a woman among women, sharing our human condition. And she goes with him, Jesus, her son, all the way to the end of the line.

Of what happened to her after Passover, we know only from a single sentence in the New Testament. It describes the Apostles meeting in Jerusalem: "with one heart, all these joined constantly in prayer together with some women, including Mary mother of Jesus, and with his brothers" (Acts 1:14).

Only then does she try to put her memories in order, meditating, entwining, weaving together all the threads of this extraordinary story. And thus— even though chronologically she is the last in this long series of women mentioned in the Bible—she becomes the first.

This surely is the deeper meaning of the dogma of the Assumption as defined by the Church, which, though there is no trace of it in the canonical Bible, sets the Virgin Mary in heaven: by the Father and with her Son.

NOTES

> **Introduction** . pp. 6–23

1. In this period, the heart was not considered the seat of feelings, but of the intelligence and the will. **- 2.** There is no word in Hebrew exactly equivalent to "body," hence the regular recourse to the term "flesh." **- 3.** It is often forgotten that God, if He curses and punishes Cain following his murder of Abel, also protected him: "Yahweh [said], 'Whoever kills Cain will suffer a sevenfold vengeance.' So Yahweh put a mark on Cain, so that no one coming across him would kill him" (Genesis 4:11–16). The biblical story, moreover, relates how Cain built cities and had many descendants. **- 4.** There exists, however, one exception; that of the cunning Jacob, the third of the great patriarchs. Misled by his father-in-law, Laban, he subsequently became rich at the latter's expense, to the point that his brothers-in-law became envious and Laban himself betrayed his annoyance. Thus Yahweh advises Jacob to leave: "Go back to the land of your ancestors, where you were born, and I shall be with you" (Genesis 31:3). Before taking this advice, Jacob called his wives, Rachel and Leah (see below, p. 39), and told them the whole story. They also think it better he make his escape on the camels (Genesis 31:14–17). **- 5.** Quoted by Giulia Sissa, in Georges Duby and Michelle Perrot, eds., *A History of Women in the West: From Ancient Goddesses to Christian Saints* (Cambridge, MA: Harvard University Press, 1993), 67 and 69 (originally published in Italian, Rome: Guislaterza, 1990). **- 6.** A text of rabbinical origin practically synonymous with the Torah, the Law. It is founded on the written, "Mosaic" observance, based on the first five books in the Bible (that is, the Pentateuch), and on the oral law handed down from master to pupil, providing precise definitions as to how written statutes are to be enforced. **- 7.** Ancient Judaism allowed slavery but greatly limited its use and imposed a large number of obligations on masters. For example, he could not subject slaves to "degrading" tasks and had to provide them with food of similar quality to his own, etc. The status of slaves can be gathered from this verse in Deuteronomy (the fifth and last book of the Pentateuch that comments on and clarifies the preceding): "Remember that you were once a slave in Egypt and that Yahweh your God redeemed you; that is why I am giving you this order today" (Deuteronomy 15:15). In other words: Treat them as you would like to be treated. **- 8.** Edited by Geoffrey Wigoder (New York: New York University Press, 2002 [1989]). **- 9.** Josy Eisenberg, *La Femme au temps de la Bible* (Paris: Stock, 1993).

> **Mothers** . pp. 24–51

1. Like Jacob, he will have twelve sons, the ancestors of the twelve Arab tribes **- 2.** Though the Apostle Paul, going back to the lesson of the rabbis, fails to mention the two boys playing, in the Letter to the Galatians (Galatians 4:29) he observes that "the child born in the way of human nature persecuted the child born through the Spirit." **- 3.** André Chouraqui's version of this passage runs (in translation): "Yahweh held me back from giving birth" (*En tête* [Paris: J.-C. Lattès, 1992]). **- 4.** Cf. Jacques Le Goff, *Un long Moyen Âge* (Paris: Tallandier, 2004). **- 5.** He had tried, the text notes, to take his "sons-in-law" along with him, but they thought it was a joke. Clearly, biblical authors sometimes mixed up marriage and engagement, and the two virgin girls were already betrothed. - **6.** *Aqeb*, however, also means "brother," and *Ya aqeb* can be translated by "whom God protects." - **7.** A people from Asia Minor, whose relations with Israel were complicated. - **8.** Marriage with two sisters was prohibited at the time of Moses. - **9.** The custom in the Upper Mesopotamian region was that part of the sum the fiancé donated to the father at the wedding was made over to the wife. But in the case of Laban, who, in place of a dowry, had obliged Jacob to work for him for fourteen years, it was the father alone who benefited. - **10.** A prostitute was not allowed to "launder" the money she earned by offering it as a sacrifice, and also could not, unlike a divorcée, marry a priest.

> **Heroines and Protectors** . pp. 52–71
1. The Bible sometimes calls Yahweh by this term. - **2.** Cf. Josy Eisenberg, *La Femme au temps de la Bible* (Paris: Stock, 1993). - **3.** The other being a certain Caleb, who, like Moses and Joshua, never wavered from his trust in God's pledge. - **4.** The book of Judith does not appear in the Hebrew nor the Protestant Bible. It was admitted to the Roman Catholic Bible at a late date: in the West, it appears in official lists from the time of the Roman synod of 382 CE and in the East from the Council of Constantinople of 692.

> **The Prophetesses** . pp. 72–85
1. Moses occupies a special place among the prophets because he spoke with Yahweh "face to face as a man talks to his friend" (Exodus 33:11), and also because of his historical role, from the exodus from Egypt to the frontier of the Promised Land. - **2.** Josy Eisenberg, *La Femme au temps de la Bible*. - **3.** Hazor, the most extensive archaeological site in Israel (seventy-seven hectares), includes a Canaanite acropolis and a vast altar. - **4.** Her name was, however, given to two of the Temple's gates.

> **The Queens** . pp. 86–103
1. Several translations of this passage are possible. The one in the text is taken from rabbi and historian Josy Eisenberg's *La Femme au temps de la Bible*, which mirrors the debate concerning the episode that preoccupied the rabbinical community. The New Jerusalem Bible, which this volume usually follows, has "if this is too little, I shall give you other things as well." André Chouraqui's translation (an exegete who was also deputy mayor of Jerusalem; French ed. Desclées de Brouwer, 1985) has (in English): "And if this is too little, I'll add some more here and there." If we employ the translation quoted by J. Eisenberg, it is because it gives a clearer sense of the deliberations of the rabbis, without altering the core meaning of the prophet's remarks. - **2.** The Ammonites, descendants of one of Lot's daughters, often engaged in wars against the Israelites. - **3.** One of the honorifics of the emperor of Ethiopia was "the victorious Lion of the tribe of Judah." - **4.** The Hebrew Bible places this tale—probably written in the mid-second century BCE—among the historical books, as distinguished from those constituting the Law and the Prophets. The account given there is a brief one and the book of Esther in the Protestant Bible follows it. The Catholic Bible on the other hand incorporates supplementary material in ancient Greek.

PHOTOGRAPHIC CREDITS:

© akg-images: pp. 16–17, 29, 31, 32–33, 41, 58, 60–61, 78, 81, 97, 103, 116, 117, 122, 134, 144, 146–47, 148, 152; © akg-images/ © ADAGP: p. 30, 54; © akg-images/Cameraphoto: pp. 10–11, 43, 84, 94–95, 143; © akg-images/Electa: p. 20, 106; © akg-images/Erich Lessing: pp. 24–25, 26, 34–35, 37, 42, 46–47, 52–53, 57, 69, 82–83, 86–87, 98, 99, 100, 109, 114–15, 118, 128–29, 130–31, 135, 136, 137, 142; © akg-images/Laurent Lecas: p. 111; © akg-images/Nimatallah: p. 51, 74; © akg-images/Pietro Baguzzi/© All rights reserved: p. 125; © akg-images/Rabatti-Domingie: p. 85, 126; © British Library/akg-images: pp. 72–73; © Wilfried Bahnmüller – ARTOTHEK: p. 77; © Blauel/ Gnamm – ARTOTHEK: p. 88; © Giraudon/The Bridgeman Art Library: p. 67, 79; © Peter Willi/The Bridgeman Art Library: p. 6; © Leemage: p. 121; © Angelo/Leemage: p. 139; © Costa/Leemage: p. 45; © Electa/ Leemage /© All rights reserved: p. 151; © Fototeca/Leemage: p. 63; © Heritage Images/Leemage: p. 48; © Ravenna/Leemage: p. 101; © RMN – Gérard Blot : p. 112; © RMN – Gérard Blot/© ADAGP: p. 64; © RMN – Hervé Lewandowski: p. 123, 140; © RMN (Musée d'Orsay) – Hervé Lewandowski/© ADAGP: p. 132; © RMN – Thierry Le Mage/ © Succession Picasso – Gestion droits d'auteur: p. 92; © BPK, Berlin, Dist RMN – Dietmar Katz: p. 91; © The National Gallery, London, Dist. RMN/National Gallery Photographic Department: p. 12; © The Metropolitan Museum of Art, Dist. RMN/image of the MMA: p. 70; © The National Gallery, London/Scala, Florence: p. 38; © Musée des Beaux-Arts de Dole, cl. Henri Bertand: pp. 104–05.

COVER:

Hermann Anschuetz, *Esther*, Pushkin Museum, Moscow
© Bridgeman Giraudon

Translated from the French by David Radzinowicz
Design: Julianne Cordes and Corinne Dury
Copyediting: Penny Isaac
Typesetting: Anne-Lou Bissières
Proofreading: Chrisoula Petridis
Color Separation: Quat'Coul, Paris
Printed in Italy by Graphart

Distributed in North America
by Rizzoli International Publications, Inc.

Simultaneously published in French as *Femmes de la Bible*
© Flammarion, Paris, 2010

English-language edition
© Flammarion, Paris, 2010

10 11 12   3 2 1

ISBN: 978-2-08-030156-7

Dépôt légal: 10/2010